25 W

THE
CHILTERNS

£1

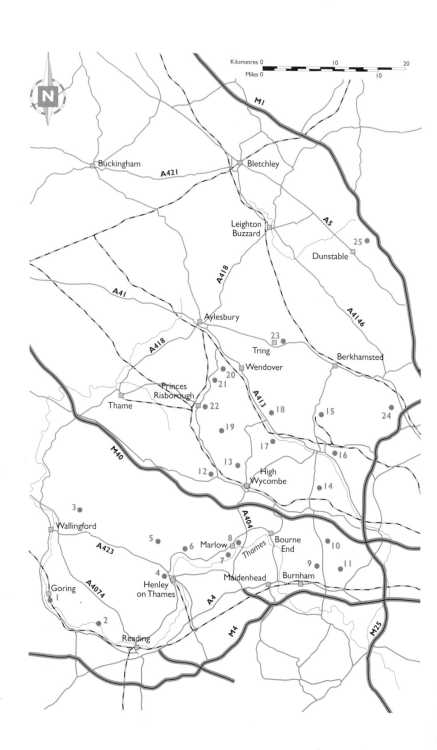

Kilometres 0 · · · 10 · · · 20
Miles 0 · · · 10

N

M1

Buckingham
A421
Bletchley

Leighton
Buzzard
A5
Dunstable 25

A418
A41
Aylesbury
A4146

A418
23
Tring
Wendover
Berkhamsted

20
Princes
Risborough 21
Thame 22
A413
18
15
24

M40
19
17
13
High
Wycombe 16
12
14

3
Wallingford
A404
5 8
Marlow Bourne
A423 6 Thames End 10
7
Maidenhead
4 9 11
Henley Burnham
Goring on Thames
1 A4074 A4
2
M4
Reading
M25

25 WALKS

THE CHILTERNS

Leigh Hatts

Series Editor: Roger Smith

THE STATIONERY OFFICE

Applications for reproduction should be made to The Stationery Office

Acknowledgements

The Stationery Office Limited acknowledge with thanks access to and use of photographs from Leigh Hatts.

British Library Cataloguing in Publication Data

A catalogue record for this book is available from the British Library

ISBN 0 11 495727 4

CONTENTS

USEFUL INFORMATION

The Chilterns are within the area covered by the Southern Tourist Board, which can be contacted at 40 Chamberlayne Road, Eastleigh, Hampshire SO5 5JH (01703 620006). Tourist Information Centres can be found at the following locations:

Amersham: Tesco car park, London Road West HP7 OAH, 01494 729492, open Apr-Sept.

Dunstable: The Library, Vernon Place LU5 4HA, 01582 471012, open Easter-Oct.

Henley: Town Hall, Market Place RG9 2AQ, 01491 578034, open Easter-Oct.

Marlow: Pound Lane SL7 2AE, 01628 483597. open Easter-Oct.

Wendover: The Clock Tower, High Street HP22 6DU, 01296 696759, open Easter-Oct.

The main Tourist Information Centres for the southern Chilterns are at::

Maidenhead: The Library, St Ives Road SL6 1QU, 01628 781110.

Windsor: Central Station, Thames Street SL4 1PJ, 01753 852010.

Public Transport

The main railway companies serving the Chilterns are Chiltern Railways (London Marylebone to Aylesbury and Birmingham, 0990 165165, national call rate) and Thames Trains (London Paddington to Reading and Oxford, 0171 262 6767).

Berkshire, Buckinghamshire and Oxfordshire county councils publish their own bus information to co-ordinate services within the county. Berkshire's Passenger Transport Unit answers enquiries on 01734 234524. Buckinghamshire operates a local call rate

METRIC MEASUREMENTS

At the beginning of each walk, the distance is given in miles and kilometres. Within the text, all measurements are metric for simplicity (and indeed our Ordnance Survey maps are now all metric). However, it was felt that a conversion table might be useful to those readers who still tend to think in Imperial terms.

The basic statistic to remember is that one kilometre is five-eighths of a mile. Half a mile is equivalent to 800 metres and a quarter-mile is 400 metres. Below that distance, yards and metres are little different in practical terms.

km	miles
1	0.625
1.6	1
2	1.25
3	1.875
3.2	2
4	2.5
4.8	3
5	3.125
6	3.75
6.4	4
7	4.375
8	5
9	5.625
10	6.25
16	10

Travel Line on 0345 382000. Oxfordshire County Council can be contacted on 01865 810405. Local timetable booklets are usually available at Tourist Information Centres.

The main bus companies serving the Chilterns are:

Beeline, 01753 524144

Chiltern Queens, 01491 680354

Chilternrover, 0345 788788

Aylesbury & the Vale, 0345 788788

Oxford Bus Company, 01865 711312

Green Line, 0181 688 7261

Wycombe Bus Company, 01494 520941

Reading Buses, 01273 450 9509

Luton and Dunstable, 0345 788788

Ordnance Survey Maps

Many of the walks can be followed on the OS Chiltern Hills North (Explorer 2) and Chiltern Hills South (Explorer 3) maps. These maps, replacing in the Chilterns the Pathfinder Series, are at 1:25,000 scale and contain useful additional information.

The Chiltern Society

Thanks to the Chiltern Society as much as local authorities, the path network will usually be found to be in good order whether you are in woodland, farmland, open chalk grassland or on a village outskirts. Chiltern Society footpath maps, published by Shire Publications and available at bookshops and tourist information centres, are as good a companion as (some say better than) an OS Pathfinder map.

INTRODUCTION

This book describes 25 walks in the area bounded roughly by the Icknield Way to the north, the River Thames to the south and west and the Grand Union Canal to the east. Buckinghamshire, Oxfordshire, Hertfordshire and even a corner of Bedfordshire contribute to the countryside known as the Chilterns. The Chilterns Area of Outstanding National Beauty (AONB) covering 880 sq km and the Chiltern Hundreds do not share exactly the same boundaries, so the extent of the Chilterns is always a matter of opinion, but at the heart of the Chilterns are the Chiltern Hills.

In writing the book I have kept in mind the visitor who is not an experienced hillwalker, so that the recommended route to the summit of Coombe Hill is, for example, a gentle climb with the steep path used for a descent. Many of the walks are short and none is longer than 13 kilometres (8 miles). They could be a good introduction to the pleasure of walking for both children and adults.

Dr William Bird chose the Chilterns for the Countryside Commission-backed Health Walks experiment, which has proved that walking can contribute towards good health. He says that walkers should exert themselves enough to become slightly breathless but not so much as to interfere with conversation.

Dr Bird also suggests that looking at local history and the natural habitat should be part of the holistic experience. This is the countryside of Milton, Gray and Rupert Brooke. I have tried to emphasise places of historical interest locked away in the hills and preserved for us due to the protection of surrounding high ground. Both the Reformation and the Civil War missed several fine buildings, although in another part of the area a key struggle against Charles I was played out by the Roundheads. Quiet dissent by Chartists and Quakers was a little easier hidden in the Chiltern hills than in London.

Most of the walks can be reached by public transport. The Metropolitan Underground Line, the Chiltern Lines and Thames Trains all provide a fast railway service out of central London. Sadly, Chiltern residents have one of the highest car ownership levels in the country, but moves to check the growth in traffic include continuing the improvement in public transport. The Chiltern Standing Conference, concerned with the well-being of the AONB, is also looking at the promotion of public transport. A walk is certainly improved if you can both avoid traffic and be carried home swiftly without having to worry about the driving.

Special clothing is not generally required for walking but the information at the beginning of each walk sometimes advises strong footwear. If you complete all the walks you will have enjoyed some of the finest examples of the Chilterns' diverse countryside.

Afterwards you may be inspired to explore further; the number of footpaths is staggering, and the wide choice of possibilities has for me been the hardest part of compiling this book.

Leigh Hatts

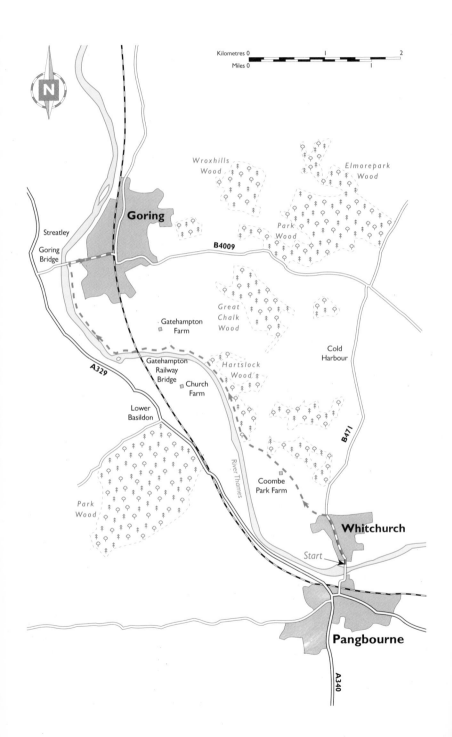

Kilometres 0   1   2

Miles 0   1

N

Wroxhills Wood

Elmorepark Wood

Goring

Streatley

Goring Bridge

B4009

Park Wood

Gatehampton Farm

Great Chalk Wood

A329

Gatehampton Railway Bridge

Church Farm

Cold Harbour

Hartslock Wood

Lower Basildon

B471

Park Wood

River Thames

Coombe Park Farm

Start

Whitchurch

Pangbourne

A340

HARTSLOCK WOOD

The Thames Path runs all the way from London to Gloucestershire, but only here in the Chilterns does it offer such a high view down onto the river. The national trail runs up into a Chiltern wood before turning north to the spectacular Goring Gap, where two villages in different counties face each other across the water and the Ridgeway enters the Chilterns. By the river at Gatehampton there is no shortage of wildfowl, thanks to the proximity of the Childe-Beale Wildlife Trust on the Berkshire bank.

This walk, which follows a short stretch of the Thames Path, begins on Whitchurch Bridge linking Pangbourne in Berkshire, which has the transport links, with Whitchurch on the Oxfordshire bank. The bridge was opened in 1901 and is one of only two on

Weir by Whitchurch Bridge.

the Thames maintaining tolls. Pedestrians, sheep, boars and pigs used to be charged one shilling and twopence (6p) each but since decimalisation, walkers have crossed free.

Cross the bridge, and on on the Whitchurch side go left to enter the driveway to The Mill, which is mentioned in Domesday Book. Beyond the cottage, turn right up a walled footpath running under a vine to the church dating from Norman times but now largely Victorian. A north aisle window shows Jesus at work with a saw in his step-father's workshop. Nearby is a monument to Richard Lybbe of Hardwick.

Goring.

Beyond the lychgate, keep forward to return to the road, and turn left to pass The Greyhound and climb the hill. After the pavement ends, keep ahead to pass the White House and go left where signs point to Long Acre Farm and Goring.

Follow the track to where the way bends left to Hartslock Farm. Here continue ahead down a stepped path into a valley. The enclosed path climbs up between fields. On entering Hartslock Wood, follow a winding path which is later briefly on a chalk cliff with a sheer drop. This affords the first good view of the river and islands where there was a primitive 'flash lock' as early as the 12th century. Before the invention of the now familiar 'pound' lock, wooden paddles would be removed from a weir to allow a barge to go downstream with the water flow or be dragged through.

The woodland path runs along a shelf on the hillside, and as the path descends through the beech trees and old yews there are more river views. Across the water is the towpath and lonely 13th-century Basildon Church with a tower added in 1734, just seven years before pioneer agriculturalist Jethro Tull was buried in the churchyard. Born at Basildon, he was educated at Oxford University and brought many innovations into farming. One of his main inventions was the seed-drill, which enabled seeds to be sown in straight rows. He could not, however, have foreseen that in the 1970s his name would be taken by a pop group!

Where the ground levels out, the path becomes enclosed as it runs along the side of a field and a little way from the river. Just before reaching a tall hedge at Gatehampton Farm, go left on a path to reach Ferry Cottage beyond a backwater bridge. This is where the towpath crossed the river and towing horses had to be ferried. Apart from the cottage and trains on the nearby Gatehampton Bridge this is a quiet place, although Stone Age and Roman relics found here suggest it was an important crossing from earliest times.

Go under the 1839 Brunel railway bridge and, after some distance, through a kissing gate. The Goring Gap hills can be seen half-right. As the ground indicates, many walkers cut the corner although obviously the towpath stays with the riverbank. After a stile, the path leaves the fields and passes three well spaced and charming boathouses. There is a fine view of Streatley Bridge before the path passes the grass picnic area and the moorings. From here there is another grand view of the large Ferry Cottage where Oscar Wilde stayed in 1893 - his play *An Ideal Husband* includes such characters as Viscount Goring and Countess Basildon. Sir Arthur 'Bomber' Harris of World War Two Bomber Command fame lived at the house in later years, and died there at the age of 92 in 1984.

Hartslock Wood cliff-top path.

Cross the mill stream and turn right to walk up the main street of Goring, passing the church, which was once part of a convent, and The Miller of Mansfield in Station Road.

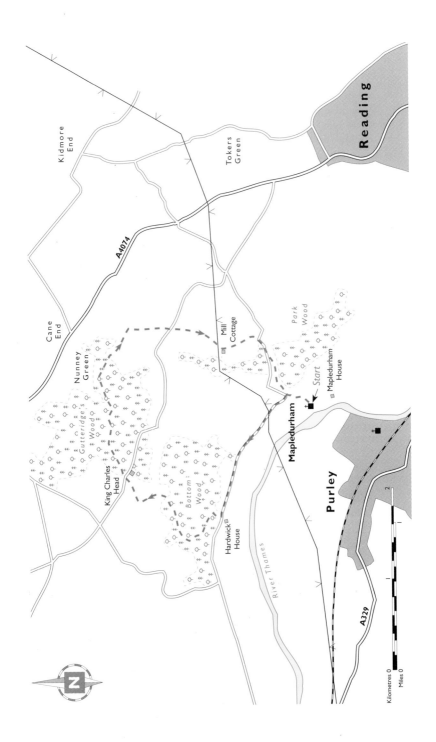

Reading

Kidmore End

Tokers Green

A4074

Cane End

Park Wood

Nunney Green

Mill Cottage

Start

Mapledurham House

Gutteridge's Wood

Mapledurham

King Charles Head

Bottom Wood

Purley

Hardwick House

River Thames

A329

Kilometres 0
Miles 0

1   2

MAPLEDURHAM

lexander Pope's poetry makes reference to Mapledurham, which means 'settlement by the stream and maples'. Later it was a setting for John Galsworthy's *Forsyte Saga*. There has been a mill here since at least Norman times and the present 500-year-old building, the last working mill on the Thames, supplies flour to nearby bakeries - and visitors. The 15th-century church by the mill stream has a tower clock given by William IV whose son, by actress Mrs Jordan, was vicar here. The south aisle survived the Reformation to remain in the ownership of the Roman Catholic family at Mapledurham House.

The mansion, built in Armada year 1588, is occupied by the family who maintained the Old Faith, and a cluster of shells above a dormer window confirms that it is a Catholic house - there is a priest's hole and the discreet private chapel at the back can be seen from the churchyard. The house faces east and not towards the river because physician and traveller Andrew Boorde had once warned: "The South wynde doth corrupt and doth make evyl vapours." Among films and TV programmes partly shot here are *The Eagle Has Landed*, *Inspector Morse* and *Class Act*.

Walk away from the river and out of the village to reach the White House on the left. At the cottage, go left on a track along the side of the valley. From the rising chalky path there are views down onto the Thames. In early summer the way is fringed by cow

INFORMATION

Distance: 8km (5 miles).

Start and finish: Mapledurham Church car park.

Terrain: Road and path. Some sections muddy in wet weather. Boots or strong shoes recommended.

Refreshments: The King Charles Head, Guttridge's Wood. Teas are served in the Old Manor in the Mapledurham House grounds on summer weekends from 1400 to 1700. Entry via house car park entrance at north end of village.

Public transport: Riverbus from Reading at 14.00 on summer weekends (01734 481088). Return boat leaves from behind mill at 17.00, so you would need to walk briskly.

Opening hours: *Mapledurham House:* Easter Day to Sep: Sat, Sun & Bank Holidays 1430-1700. Admission charge.

Mapledurham Watermill: Easter-Sep: Sat & Sun 1300-1700; Oct-Palm Sun 1400-1600.

Wood around Hardwick House from River Thames.

parsley. After ornamental gates, the path passes East Lodge which is the entrance to the Hardwick House estate. There is another view before the path runs behind the Tudor mansion where Elizabeth I stayed. Charles I played bowls on the lawn running down to the Thames towards the end of his troubled reign, and the house suffered damage in the Civil War. Hardwick House is now the residence of Sir Julian Rose who runs the 300- acre Hardwick Organic Farm, noted for its unpasteurised milk.

On reaching a junction of paths just beyond the house, bear right with the iron fence up into Bottom

Wood. Ignore a side path and follow the main track as it bears right to climb the wooded hill. There are occasional views over the Thames. On turning north over a crosspath, the path passes a pit on the left and a right turning before continuing straight ahead. At a four-way junction go right - as suggested by the arrow on the tree.

The path curves to the left as it loses height. Before the way curves left again, leave the main track to go ahead up through the trees. The path, used by horses, rises to reach a stile. Do not go over this stile but bear left to find another. Walk up the side of a

Hardwick House from River Thames.

field and go through a small gate on the right leading to a metalled road by Holly Copse.

Turn left up the road to pass Briar Cottage and the entrance to Rose Cottage. On approaching a gate by New Cottages (there may be a boat opposite) go right over a stile. Keep ahead along the side of the field (Collisend Common). At the next field boundary there is a hidden stile. Still keep forward to a stile by a gate at a road. Along to the right can be seen the King

Charles Head sign. On the pub's frontage are lines
written in 1647 when the King was at Hardwick
House.

The walk continues on the far side of the road on a
bridleway which runs half right into Gutteridge's
Wood. Stay on the main path, which becomes more
defined. When, after a dip, the path divides, take the
right fork. At a road go left, past a partly hidden
thatched cottage. There are sometimes fingersticks
and plants on sale at Foxgloves.

At the end of the road go ahead into Nunney Wood.
When the bridleway runs into the open by a field
there is a view half right up to Cross Lanes Orchard.
At the end of the field turn right down a hollow
lane which curves left with another view of apple
trees up on the hill. At a junction bear right uphill
on a path which runs alongside Cross Lanes
Orchard, planted in 1948 and one of the last
working orchards in the Chilterns. The oldest trees
are Ellinson's Orange but the five-acre site now has
30 varieties including Egremont Russet. Apples are
on sale at the farm shop from August to December,
and you may well find them irresistible. The path
meets a road at the Cross Lanes entrance.

Keep forward down the
open road opposite. At a
bend in the road pass
Mill Farm, where the
thatched Mill Cottage
building, dating from
1335, is England's oldest
cottage. Keep right at a
junction to reach Step
Cottage. Turn left into a
field and half right to
walk up the field towards the far end of the wood. Go

Mill Cottage.

through a field gap and bear right downhill to a stile
and steps leading to the road in Mapledurham. Turn
left for the village.

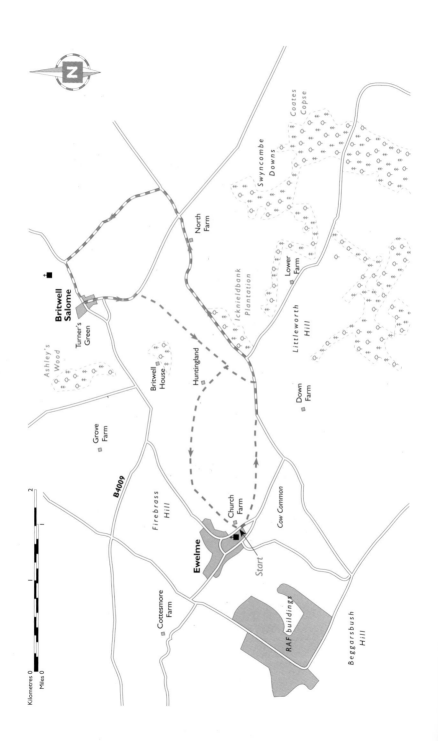

EWELME AND BRITWELL SALOME

Ewelme and Britwell Salome are remote unspoilt villages on a stretch of the Ridgeway where the hills are gentle but still provide good views of the varied countryside rich in landscape and heritage.

Ewelme is a long village with a pub, post office and village pond feeding the Ewelme Brook. Until recently its pure and sparkling water passed through watercress beds before becoming one of the many Thames tributaries. The village is so hidden that it escaped the damaging attentions of both Henry VIII and the Roundheads.

The early 15th-century church retains a rood screen and a rare tall font cover. Its cloister is still used by a small community founded by Chaucer's granddaughter Alice, Countess of Suffolk, whose tomb shows her both in life and emaciated by death. The attractive church was used for filming John Mortimer's *Paradise Postponed* in which the Rector is called Simeon Simcox - a Henry Simcox was incumbent here in the 1890s. The cloister which always has a resident cat, is featured in Cynthia Harnett's children's book *The Writing on the Hearth*. The school to the south is the oldest state school still in its original building, erected in 1437, three years before Eton was founded.

The walk starts outside the east end of Ewelme Church in Parson's Lane. Leave the churchyard, where *Three Men in a Boat* author Jerome K. Jerome is buried on the east side, by one of the gateways on to Parson's Lane and turn right to pass the Old Rectory. After a short distance, bear left up a rough track. The way bends and narrows before running across a field with

INFORMATION

Distance: 10km (6 miles).

Start and finish: Ewelme Church.

Terrain: Roads, tracks and paths. No special footwear needed.

Refreshments: The Red Lion at Ewelme. Teas at Ewelme School on second Sunday of month, Apr-Oct except Aug, 1500-1800.

Public Transport: Bus from Wallingford.

Tourist Information: 01491 826550.

Cat in Ewelme cloister.

Ewelme School.

views of the rolling hills. Behind can be seen Wittenham Clumps above the Thames at Dorchester and Didcot Power Station.

There are two stiles at field boundaries before the way drops down to a stile by the road at Warren Bottom. Turn left along the road to pass a bridleway entrance on the left. (To shorten the walk, go left at a bridleway sign a few yards further on, and left again at a junction to join the end of the route.) A little further on the road is joined from the right by the Swan's Way, a 105km bridleway linking Salcey Forest near Milton Keynes with Goring-on-Thames. Where the road swings right, keep ahead up a chalk track alongside a wood.

The path is part of the Ridgeway or Icknield Way, and the wood is known as the Icknield Bank Plantation. Soon there is a view over to the left of Britwell House and the monument in the grounds. The small mansion was built in 1727 for a bachelor. The numerous owners since have included designer David Hicks and his wife Lady Pamela, daughter of Lord Mountbatten, who lived there in the 1960s and 1970s.

The way bends to pass North Farm, where the Ridgeway National Trail joins the original route from the right. The path continues over a road and after 350m reaches a junction of paths. Here turn sharp left through a tunnel of trees running north. At the far end there is a brief glimpse, half right, of the church tower at Watlington. The path continues down to a road by Cooper's Farm on the edge of Britwell Salome.

Go left along the road to find, round the wooded bend, the white painted Britwell Priory dating from the 12th century, when it belonged to Canterbury

Cathedral. The lane at the side leads up to the church which dates from the 13th century, when the village was known as 'Bruttewell Sulham'. The huge former rectory next door is Georgian with an earlier half-timbered wing. The Rev J.C. Mansfield lived there for 50 years from 1897. Among his recreations were playing the fiddle, keeping bees and maintaining a Kerry cow.

But the walk continues ahead uphill on the main village road, passing the grain store (right) to a crossroads by the Red Lion. Turn left at the pub. Just before the turning to the Old Post Office there is a many sided house on the right. Keep ahead, and as the road becomes enclosed, bear right down a rough track. There is a lodge in the distance. Beyond the house, the way runs ahead along the back of Britwell House, which can be seen through trees on the right.

Continue ahead on the wide gravel track (ignore a left turn) to a T-junction (where the short cut joins from the field ahead). Turn right to go uphill past Huntingland pig farm. As the path levels out at the

Path to Britwell Salome.

top, there is a view ahead of Wittenham Clumps. Where the main track swings left, keep forward. There is a wood over to the right.

Before reaching a road, go over a stile on the left (many use the gate). Go half right up the hill to a stile at a corner. Keep ahead on the enclosed path at the side of the field. At the far end the way runs down to Church Farm. Continue ahead to Parson's Lane. Ewelme Church is opposite.

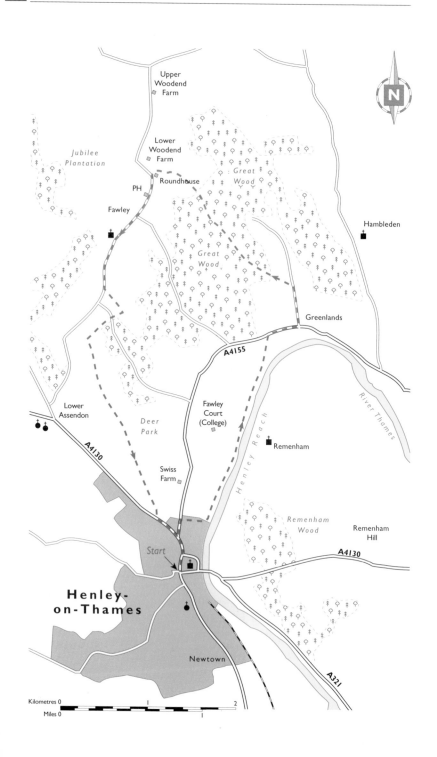

HENLEY AND FAWLEY

One of the finest views of the Chiltern hills is from the riverside at Henley. This walk does not use the famous towpath, but instead follows the less well known path on the Oxfordshire bank of the Thames which marks the boundary of the Chilterns. A wooded hill path takes the walk up to a scattered village on a ridge above the town.

The way out of Henley is along Bell Street from the Market Place. Keep on the right until the street becomes Northfield End, just before the main road forks. On a wall to the right is a plaque recalling Rupert's Elm, where Prince Rupert had a Parliamentary spy's body exhibited as a warning to Roundhead supporters during the winter of 1642-43.

INFORMATION

Distance: 12 km (7 1/2 miles).

Start and finish: Henley Bridge.

Terrain: Roads, tracks and paths. No special footwear needed.

Refreshments: Wide choice of cafés and bakeries in Henley. The Walnut Tree, Fawley.

Public Transport: Rail to Henley Station.

Take the right hand road and just beyond the lodges and Phyllis Court, go right down a wide footpath to find the river beyond a gate. The path runs half left between the fences to the bank to go downstream and over a footbridge.

Later, a narrow footbridge takes the path over a canal and under a wall, which is on the Oxfordshire-Buckinghamshire boundary, and over more water to the grounds of Fawley Court. The mansion, begun in 1684 for merchant William Freeman, has been known as 'Poland-on-Thames' since 1953, when it became a school for sons of exiled Poles.

Oxfordshire-Bucks boundary at Fawley Court.

After crossing the main canal in front of the house, keep ahead rather than hugging the riverbank. The way crosses a couple more channels before passing Temple Island with its fishing lodge by Wyatt, built in 1771 as a focus for the vista from Fawley Court where the garden was landscaped by Capability Brown.

After another footbridge, the river bends west as the path begins to swing a little left. A boarded path runs

Temple Island.

through a strip of woodland bounded by streams. The path continues slightly at an angle to a final footbridge before crossing the drive of Greenlands, once home of bookseller W.H. Smith (1825-91), whose business greatly expanded after he gained permission to sell books and newspapers at railway stations. He entered parliament in 1868 and from 1877-80 was First Lord of the Admiralty. In this role he was the inspiration for the "Ruler of the Queen's Navee" in Gilbert and Sullivan's operetta *HMS Pinafore*. The house can be seen to the right. A stile leads to the main road.

Go right along the pavement to pass near the house and take the second turning on the right known as Dairy Lane. (The pavement ends opposite but it is advisable to cross in advance as the junction is on a dangerous corner.)

The lane runs straight ahead, passing cottages with Smith's WHS initials above the door. After the second double cottage, take the second turning on the left. Where the path divides, bear right up the steep field to enter Great Wood. The path is at first steep but later the ground levels out as it runs through the beech wood.

Keep ahead ignoring all turnings until, some distance

Roundhouse at Fawley.

beyond a gateway, arrows on trees indicate a double bend. The ground rises gently and on coming level with a fence and into the open the way narrows. Later there is a seat by a neat hedge. The path bears left to join the track to Orchards. Just before road is the Pink Cottage and Roundhouse, a tower built as part of a farmhouse in 1730 to enhance the view from Fawley Court below.

Continue ahead down the road which runs through the scattered village of Fawley, passing The Walnut Tree pub to the right. Ignore a left turn and after the village hall keep left to pass the lychgate entrance to the Fawley churchyard.

The church's panelling, pulpit and lectern are from Cannons, the Duke of Chandos' house at Edgware. In the north transept is a Tree of Life window designed by John Piper who lived down the hill at Fawley Bottom. The second huge mausoleum outside was erected in 1752 and based on the tomb of Caecilia Metalla in Rome.

Continue along the road and past the imposing gates of the stud to the left. Where the road bends right, go left down a rough lane marked 'public footpath'. The shaded way begins to run gently downhill. Go past Last Cottage to an impressive set of red gates on the right. Here turn right down the footpath at the side. Over to the left is a large field which may have unusual animals such as llamas. To the right is a vineyard.

Go over a steep road and up the slope to a stile. Keep forward with a view over to the right of a house. After another stile the way runs steeply down and up alongside the wood on the left. Cross a track at stiles and keep forward along the edge of a field to pass back into Oxfordshire. Go over a stile to a rough lane and turn left.

This way runs ahead with various surfaces for 3km, directly down into Henley. After passing houses at Henley Park the path becomes metalled. Where this hard surface swings left, go ahead through the kissing gate to continue across farmland along the top of a ridge. The white Wargrave Manor can be seen in the distance.

After another kissing gate, still keep ahead between the lines of trees splaying out. The line of the path can often be seen in the grass. There is a fine view across Henley and left over the Thames Valley only partly blocked by trees. Go down the hill to a kissing gate on the edge of a dark wood. The path runs downhill and alongside a field to a main road. Go left past the Old White Horse to walk into Henley.

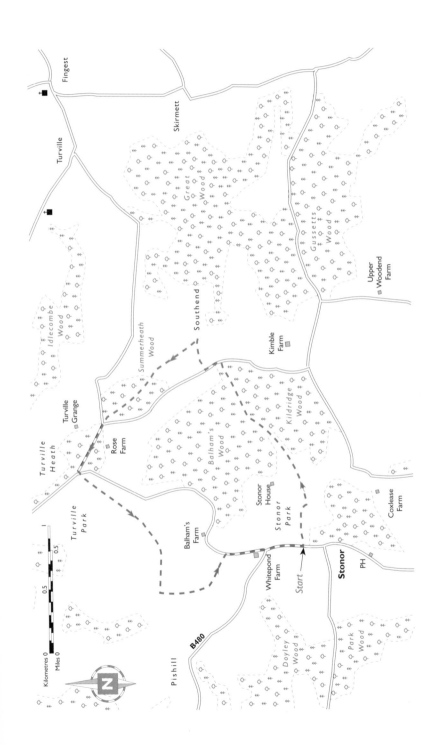

STONOR

This area on the Buckinghamshire-Oxfordshire borders is one of the most secluded and beautiful parts of the Chilterns. It is still possible to stand still on a hill and not hear any traffic. Indeed, it has long been lonely here and the history of Stonor, like Ewelme, confirms that it was forgotten and by-passed by the armies enforcing the great upheavals of the Tudor and Stuart years.

The walk starts at the north end of the village, shortly before the main gateway to Stonor Park. Go through the high iron kissing gate into the deer park. A waymark points to 'Southend'. Most of the year the path can be seen running ahead uphill through the grass.

Soon there is an early view down in the valley of Stonor House, which is so hidden and lonely that both Henry VIII's agents and the Roundheads missed it, leaving the family free to maintain its Roman Catholic chapel which can be seen at the far end of the mansion. In Elizabeth I's reign the Jesuit martyr St Edmund Campion hid here in 1581 and secretly printed his Ten Reasons pamphlet defending the Old Faith. He was captured, taken to London, tried on a

INFORMATION

Distance: 6km (4 miles).

Start and finish: Stonor Park side entrance at north end of village.

Terrain: Roads, tracks and paths. No special footwear needed.

Parking: There is limited roadside parking opposite the start of the walk.

Refreshments: The Stonor Arms, Stonor.

Public Transport: Rail to Henley Station then bus.

Opening hours: *Stonor House:* 1400-1730 Sun Apr-Sept plus Wed May-Sept, Thu Jul-Aug, Sat Aug. Admission charge.

Stonor village.

trumped-up charge of conspiracy and hanged. Flying over the south wing may be the standard of Lord Camoys whose family has been here since at least the 12th century. The first mention of the present house is 1331.

Stonor House.

After drawing level with the house, the path continues up into woodland, where there is some new planting, to a deer gate. The path continues through a pine plantation to join the central valley track. At the next junction of paths, on the Oxfordshire-Buckinghamshire boundary, keep ahead to pass two cottages and reach a road. Go left on to a road known as Drovers Lane. The house opposite the next junction is called Drovers after the inn which stood on the site until recently.

At Drovers, turn right on to the concrete road. Just before the lane begins to bear left, go over a stile on the left. The path runs ahead down the side of a field, with a magnificent view across to Turville Hill with its white windmill. At the far end of the field there is another view across a valley to Turville Court. Go over the stile and bear half left to another stile on the edge of Summerheath Wood.

Take the path half right and over a crosspath through the mainly beech wood. The winding path is waymarked with white arrows on trees. Just after passing through a break in a long bank, bear off to the left on a narrow, less-used path running through bracken. Eventually the path emerges at a road near a cottage. (If the turning is missed the road is met a little higher up - just turn left.)

Turn left to pass Turville Cottage and go between Chapel Cottage and the Old Smithy to Turville Heath. Stay on the road and still keep ahead at the first road junction where a sign points to Stonor and Henley. At the T-junction go ahead on to the rough track (signed to Saviours). Pass Turville Park Cottage on the left and at the Saviours gateway keep left to go through a kissing gate.

The path runs ahead - there is a clear tread - across the vast lawn of Saviours which can be seen to the right. Go over the stile and keep forward to another, at first hidden behind the sycamore ahead. Now bear slightly left, past a protruding field corner to find an iron kissing gate leading to a track. Turn right on to the track, which bears left. Later it ceases to be enclosed as

Looking towards Turville House from Summerheath Wood.

it runs down the side of a field with Stonor village and park coming into view. There is a stile before the way bends and passes a seat. Beyond here the path continues down the now open side of the hill to meet a valley track.

Turn left to follow the farm track to gates at a road. Turn right to pass White Pond Farm and at the main road bear left to pass the main gates of Stonor Park and walk back into Stonor village.

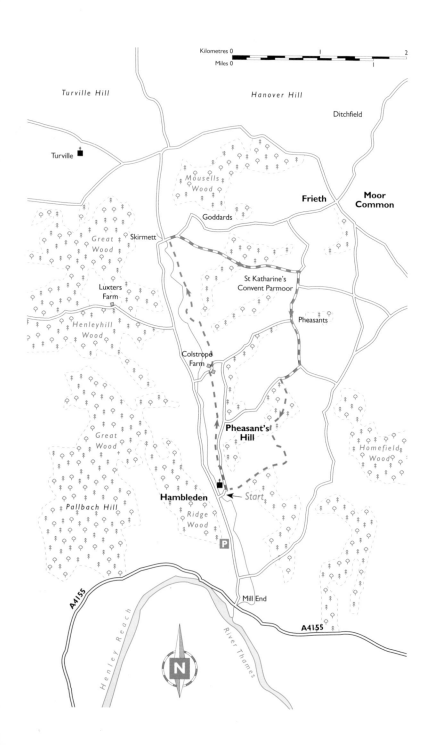

Kilometres 0   1   2

Miles 0   1

Turville Hill

Hanover Hill

Ditchfield

Turville

Mousells Wood

Frieth

Moor Common

Goddards

Skirmett

Great Wood

St Katharine's Convent Parmoor

Luxters Farm

Pheasants

Henleyhill Wood

Colstrope Farm

Great Wood

Pheasant's Hill

Homefield Wood

Pallbach Hill

Hambleden

Start

Ridge Wood

P

Mill End

A4155

Henley Reach

River Thames

A4155

N

HAMBLEDEN VALLEY

This walk, starting at the picturesque village of Hambleden, follows the Hamble Brook up the Hambleden Valley to Parmoor Convent which is on high ground amidst typical Chiltern hills.

Hambleden is so idyllic that both Joanna Trollope's *A Village Affair* and Richmal Crompton's *Just William* have been filmed here. It has also figured in the great events of English history. Lord of the manor Gilbert de Clare was one of the Magna Carta barons, and Hambleden men Adrian Scrope and Robert Deane signed Charles I's death warrant.

St Thomas de Cantelupe, who became Chancellor of England in 1264 and later Bishop of Hereford, was born here and baptised in the 12th-century font in the church. St Mary's retains some of its Norman work although the tower had to be replaced after collapsing in 1703. The Lady Chapel was known as the 'sheepfold' when shepherds sat there for the main Sunday service. The nave altar, kept in the south transept, is made from a bedhead used by Cardinal Wolsey.

The village square, with its shop and water pump under the chestnut tree, is opposite the church lychgate. At the square, turn north up the road signposted Pheasant's Hill to pass between the east end of the church and the early 17th-century Manor House, the residence of Lord Hambleden, where Charles I stayed overnight in 1646 on his way from St Albans to Oxford during the Civil War.

A short distance further go through a kissing gate on the left to follow a footpath which runs parallel to the road. Soon, over to the right, can be seen a lychgate of the new cemetery where the graves include W.H. Smith, who lived at Greenlands (see Walk 4).

Keep ahead through a series of kissing gates. The fourth, in a corner, leads to a path running

INFORMATION

Distance: 10km (6 miles).

Start and finish: Hambleden.

Terrain: Roads and steep paths. No special footwear needed.

Refreshments: Stag & Huntsman at Hambleden. The Old Crown at Skirmett. Neither welcome children.

Parking: Next to The Stag & Huntsman.

Public transport: Rail to Henley, Marlow or Reading then bus.

Opening hours: Parmoor Convent chapel and garden: 0900 to dusk.

Hambleden village.

between gardens. After the fixed gate at the far end the way follows the hedge to the right. After another kissing gate there are vines to the the right. Beyond a stile the path is by a hedge on the left. Ignore the stile to the left and keep ahead to a gate by Colstrope Farm. Keep forward to another gate at a road.

Turn right to follow the road round the bend past Little Colstrope to go ahead down a track by the entrance to Longspring House. Later the bridleway narrows before meeting a road. Go over the stile opposite to enter a field. Although the tread is often ahead the footpath runs to the left round the edge of the field and through a new copse planted in 1992 to commemorate the Queen's 40 years on the throne. Go over the stile to continue north.

Keep to the left of the lonely tree to reach a stile. Go ahead over a further field to a stile by a track leading from Anzona Farm. Continue by the gate opposite to follow the hedge on the left to a stile in the field corner. Keep forward by a line of trees and past the end of a hedge partly dividing the large field. Ahead is a stile by a gate at Skirmett.

Over to the left is the Hamble Brook which flows past the Old Crown. Once three cottages dating from 1700, the pub has two inglenook fireplaces and is packed with paintings, bottles and antiques.

Crooked Chimney Cottage, Skirmett.

The walk continues to the right along the road passing first Crooked Chimney Cottage and then Pear Tree Cottage. At the bend at the top of the hill, by the Skirmett village sign, go right up a hollow bridleway. As the path climbs there is first a view to the right down into Hambleden Valley and then a view left. Where the way divides at Hatchet Wood, keep right on the path as the ground gently rises. At the top of the hill at another junction, keep right to go ahead. After a house the way becomes metalled. Soon there is a high wall and a view of Parmoor.

The Convent of St Katharine of Alexandria moved here in 1947 after being bombed out of Fulham, south-west London, in 1945. The now small community is part of the Community of the Sue Ryder Prayer Fellowship and welcomes guests seeking a peaceful atmosphere. Visitors may call at the side door to see the chapel and the 500-year-old cedar tree. Parmoor was the childhood home of Sir Stafford Cripps-Chancellor of the Exchequer from 1947-50 and son of Lord Parmoor- and during the Second World war the exiled King Zog of Albania lived here.

The path divides at a road. Go right to pass two entrances to Parmoor and the 16th-century brick and flint Little Parmoor farmhouse. At a second junction, by a phone box at Pheasants, keep ahead down Parmoor Lane. Bear right with the main traffic at the Hambleden signpost to pass the long building of Russells Barn. Keep past a left turning and as the road begins to run down into the Hambleden Valley go left over a stile by a gate.

The path is straight until turning right into the partly beech North Close Copse. Follow the path which runs over to the south side to join a path from the left. Do not be tempted off the track by arrows pointing to the right. At a second junction again keep left. A wide path runs south to a stile by a gate. Turn left and just before another junction go over a stile on the right. The path ahead joins a concrete drive from Hutton's Farm. A well can be seen among the buildings to the left.

Cottage at Hambleden.

At a junction of farm roads ahead go right on to a path running past a small building and alongside a hedge. Beyond a stile at a wood keep ahead downhill. The way is steep and then metalled on reaching the first house in Hambleden and the turning to Kenricks -this is the former Rectory built in 1724 on the site of the house where St Thomas de Cantelupe was born. Soon there is the Stag and Huntsman, where in 1994 Anna Pasternak completed her secret book *Princess in Love*. Ahead is Hambleden village square.

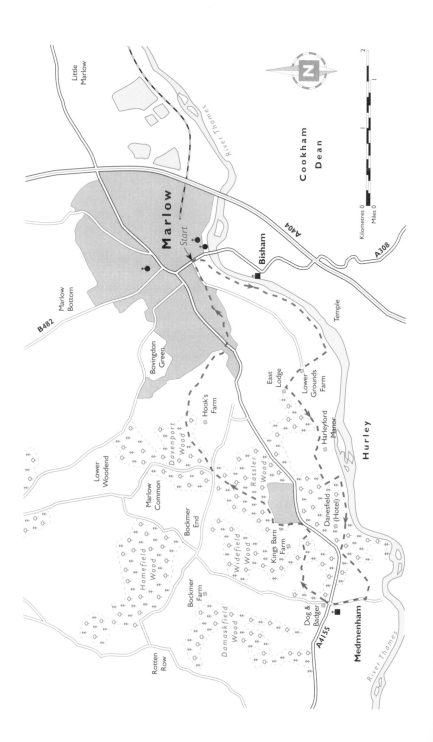

MARLOW AND MEDMENHAM

This varied walk includes the Thames towpath, a rare high cliff by the river, a tunnel and Chiltern hills. The route goes through some fine woods above the former monastic village of Medmenham, where the inn is one of the oldest in England.

Leave Marlow by going through Higginson Park gates opposite Burgers teashop on the corner of Station Road and The Causeway near the bridge. The path leads directly to the towpath which should be followed out of the town. Passing over a bridge, there is a view of Bisham Church, sometimes seen on the BBC TV weather forecast, and Bisham Abbey, founded by the Knights Templar and now the National Sports Centre. Here the towpath may have cows grazing and being watered at the Thames.

INFORMATION

Distance: 13 km (8 miles).

Start and finish: The Causeway at Marlow.

Terrain: Roads, tracks and paths. Boots or strong footwear recommended.

Refreshments: The Dog & Badger at Medmenham.

Public Transport: Rail to Marlow Station.

Cattle by the Thames.

The new houses are on Temple Mill Island, which takes its name from the Templars. Soon after the Charles Every memorial, and on drawing level with the weir, turn inland on a track. After a double bend at Lower Grounds Farm, which has a splendid barn, go through the gate to continue up to a T-junction by East Lodge.

Go left over a stile by a gate and keep forward on a straight grass path as the driveway swings away. Here the grounds of Harleyford Manor may have caravans parked in season. At the far end the path bears round and up to to the right to meet the main driveway to Harleyford Manor, built in 1755 and said to be the model for Toad Hall in *The Wind in the Willows*. Cross directly over to Harleyford Joinery and keep forward to find a notice pointing to the path continuing up steps.

At the top, cross another estate road and go ahead past a converted barn and then right, in front of two cottages. Go through the kissing gate at the side of a large gate. The way is just inside a fence until you pass a house round a bend. Go through another kissing gate to continue forward on a wide grass path. Just after the way bends right towards a farm gate, go left through a small gate. A narrow path path runs down and up through woodland.

At a junction, turn left on to a straight path which follows a wall. To the right are the grounds of Wittington which was built in 1898 for Hudson Kearley, founder of International Stores. Soon afterwards Danesfield, to the west, was rebuilt for Robert Hudson of Hudson's Soap fame. Suddenly the way drops down to run through a tunnel. At the far end there is the sound of rushing water from Hurley Weir below. The path runs steeply downhill to cross a stream and turn right by the Thames. A narrow straight path runs through woodland with water on both sides as far as a lodge.

Cross the bridge to follow a metalled drive which later passes Danesfield RAF Club. Soon there is a lodge to the left and then West Lodge to the right before the driveway meets the main road. Go forward past the Medmenham sign and at once turn left into the entrance of Abbey Lodge. Behind are long lines of poplars. Once over the main bridge in the front garden, bear right under the willow tree to a small gate. Follow the path round to the left to a stile leading into a field. Head half left to a point just to the left of the long shed on the far side. On the way the path passes two fenced trees. After a stile, keep forward to find the way fenced as it heads into trees to a gate at a footbridge. Go ahead along the narrow wooded path, keeping by a stream on the right at a junction. The path joins a wider way at the back of houses before meeting Ferry Lane in Medmenham.

A short distance to the left is a former ferry point which gives the best view of the next-door Medmenham Abbey. A 13th-century pillar is the oldest part of the restored ruins, best known as a venue

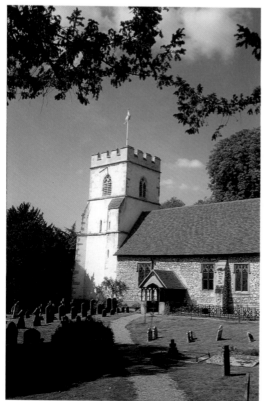

Medmenham Church.

for the profane meetings of Sir Francis Dashwood's notorious Hell Fire Club between 1750 and 1774 (see Walk 12). The ferry linked the towpath, which changes bank here.

The walk continues over the bridge, away from the river, and up Ferry Lane, passing the Old Post Office and the Manor House. In the garden of 17th-century Gillmans, just before the second bridge, can be seen the village pump.

Beyond the bridge is the church, founded by St Birinus in about 640 and rebuilt in the 12th century by Hugh de Bolebec, founder of the Abbey. The church owned the partly 14th-century Dog and Badger, and until 1899 banns of marriage were read out in the pub as well as the church. At the crossroads, go ahead to the entrance to Bockmer Lane and take the rising

Medmenham Pub.

woodland footpath on the right. These woods high above the river are a habitat for woodpeckers, tits and jays. At the top of the climb the way is through a beech wood. Where the track divides, go left to a kissing gate and turn left. Cross a drive and go ahead to another kissing gate at a road. Turn right to pass a house, the Old School.

Soon the houses end and the way becomes rough. Do not be put off by such notices as 'Private Road to The Hermitage only'. Only leave the track on approaching a gateway. Here bear left to find a path starting behind a long log. The narrow way curves down round a house behind a high fence. Soon there is a fine view down on to King's Barn Farm. After a gate the way is down a metalled lane passing the viewpoint Pheasantry Cottage.

At the bottom bear right and before reaching a main road look out for a waymark on a beech tree indicating an easily missed path on the left. Climb up through the trees on the path running north along the side of the valley. On drawing level with King's Barn Farm on the far side, look for the turning to the right to climb the hill. The way soon passes a white house before reaching a lane.

Turn left to reach Danesfield Garden Centre, where the track turns right to pass through a gateway and up towards a round white building. Here bear over to the left to find an entrance to woodland. Turn right and soon there is a good firm path running through Hog Wood. Watch for the white waymarks on trees which at two important junctions indicate a left fork. On running steeply down to a road go ahead at the road junction and right at the next to find the path continuing through the trees. Look for a waymarked divide to take the right fork and at a T-junction go right.

Soon the path runs into the open and uphill to give a fine view down Happy Valley to Bisham Abbey across the river. At the top of the hill, just before a bend, go right over a stile and along the top of the valley. The path later turns right, downhill to join the valley floor path. Here go left over a stile and head for a kissing gate by the Flint House. Follow the lane down to the main road. Go down Pound Lane opposite, which leads directly to Higginson Park and Burgers teashop on the corner of Station Road.

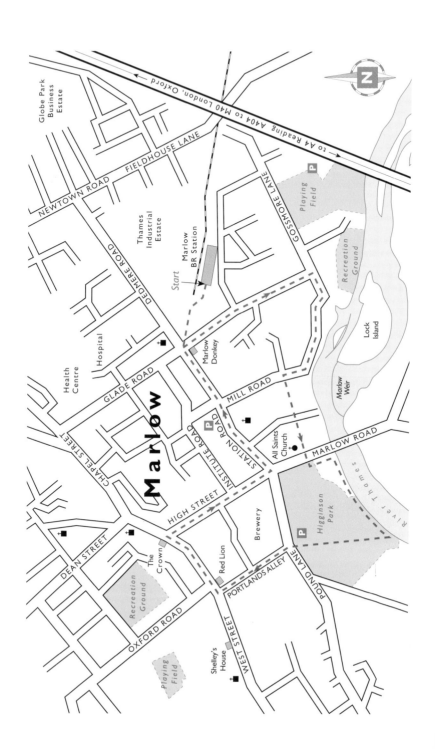

MARLOW TOWN AND RIVER

R iverside Marlow's suspension bridge is a gateway to the Chilterns. Looking down on to the small town from a hill across the Thames is the 'Wild Wood' of *The Wind in the Willows* fame, and in Marlow the literary associations include the poet Shelley, who lived here in 1817 and wrote much of *The Revolt of Islam* while drifting on the river. Meanwhile, Mary Shelley was at the house in West Street completing *Frankenstein*, the first science fiction book. The main streets are full of interesting shops and the linking alleys were known to both the Shelleys and Jerome K. Jerome, author of *Three Men in a Boat*.

INFORMATION

Distance: 4km (2 1/2 miles).

Terrain: Pavements and good paths. No special footwear needed.

Start and finish: Marlow Station.

Refreshments: Burgers teashop at The Causeway and several pubs.

From the station approach opposite the Marlow Donkey, turn down Lock Road at the side of the pub. The road runs to a T-junction with Gossmore Lane. Turn right past Vine Cottage and after a short distance the road becomes Mill Road by a footpath called Lock Road Footway.

This path, running into a riverside grassed area, is part of the Thames towpath and here until recently there was a Thames Conservancy gate. This is because the towing horses had to be brought inland while the barges were poled through the lock which can be seen, but not reached on foot, from the field.

The walk continues along Mill Road to a double bend round Marlow Mill - rebuilt in 1965 as housing. There was a mill here in Norman times and by the late 18th century there were three mills for corn, oil and England's first thimble factory. On the right is Mill House where a plaque recalls Sir Evelyn Wrench,

Marlow Church.

founder of the Royal Overseas League and the English Speaking Union. To visit the lock, go left down a passage a few yards further on.

The walk continues ahead on the road running between houses and their riverside gardens. Where the road turns inland, look for a gap in the wall on the left to turn down Seven Corners Alley, where the towing horses were led to St Peter Street. St Peter Street was the approach to Marlow Bridge until 1832.

The Two Brewers was frequented by Jerome K. Jerome, who is said to have written part of *Three Men in a Boat* there, and today is visited by the Queen's Swan Master and the Swan Uppers during the annual summer check on the Thames swans. The sign once depicted Thomas Wethered, founder of Marlow's brewery, on one side and Samuel Whitbread, whose brewery bought Wethered's, on the other. Further up the street is the 14th-century Old Parsonage next to St Peter's Roman Catholic Church, designed by Pugin of Houses of Parliament fame and completed in 1846. Its modern extension is cleverly hidden, as is the alleged hand of St James the Great, once a treasure of Reading Abbey, shown on special occasions.

From the alley, cross the road to the Old Malt House and go down a passage leading to the churchyard. All Saints was built in 1835 to replace the medieval church undermined by centuries of flooding. Cross the main bridge approach and at once go left down the far side of the bridge to find the riverside. The towpath runs past houses to moorings in front of Court Garden - a white mansion built in the 1760s for mental illness specialist Dr William Battie whose name gave us the term 'batty'.

He designed the house himself but forgot to include a staircase, which had to be added later. The grounds are called Higginson Park after Crimean War veteran Sir George Higginson, who lived here, celebrating his hundredth birthday at the house. The riverside was once a busy wharf where grain, malt and wood were loaded on barges for London.

Just before the footbridge, turn inland on a path which runs between Court Garden and the cricket ground. Follow the way to the lodge on Pound Lane. Cross over to go up the unmarked walled passage opposite. This is Portlands Alley, which meets West Street at the side of the

Shelley's house.

Red Lion. To the left is a car park on the site of satirical novelist Thomas Love Peacock's home. He was a friend of Shelley whose splendid house, marked by plaques, can be seen across the road by walking left along West Street for a short distance.

Turn back, passing the 18th-century Remnantz, the Wethered brewers family home, which housed the Royal Military Academy for for ten years from 1802 before it moved to Sandhurst. Continue past The Red Lion, staying on the same side of the road, to pass number 31, Blakes Bistro, which was known as the Old Post Office when poet T.S. Eliot lived here from 1917 to 1920. Walk up to the main road junction where the Crown looks down Marlow Road to the bridge. The pub is the former Market House, built in 1720 with an open ground floor.

Go right down the High Street. On the left, the impressive no 41 has a plaque to engineer Edwin Clark. Much earlier it had been the office of William Tierney Clark when he was building the suspension bridge in 1831. Opposite are the Wethered brewery buildings.

Burgers tea shop.

At the crossroads there is Burgers on the corner of Station Road and the Causeway. The shop has been a bakers for over 150 years. Go left along Station Road to pass Marlow Place, built in 1720 for John Wallop, later Earl of Portsmouth. Ahead at the crossroads is the Marlow Donkey and Marlow Station.

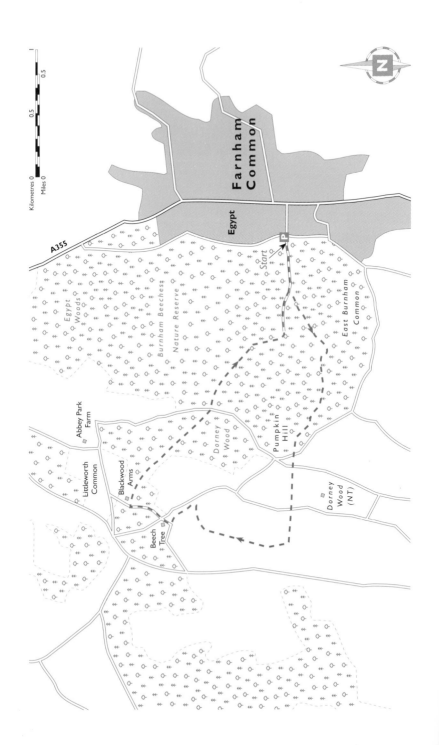

Kilometres 0
Miles 0
0.5
0.5

A355

Egypt Woods

Burnham Beeches

Nature Reserve

Farnham Common

Egypt

Start

P

East Burnham Common

Abbey Park Farm

Littleworth Common

Blackwood Arms

Beech Tree

Dorney Wood

Pumpkin Hill

Dorney Wood (NT)

BURNHAM BEECHES

The rich and diverse 240 hectare (600-acre) ancient woodland of Burnham Beeches has been maintained by the Corporation of London since 1880. The City's Coal, Corn and Finance Committee took speedy action to purchase the area, already popular with Londoners seeking fresh air, when naturalist Francis George Heath alerted the Lord Mayor of London to the sale of the woodland as building plots.

Keep the car park to the left to walk down Lord Mayor's Drive and pass The Glades tea hut before the road divides. Turn right and follow the road through a gateway and round the corner. After a short distance, and before a 'sleeping policeman' and the hill, bear half-left off the road at posts to go on to a forest path. The way bears round to the right to become a clear track through the oaks and beeches.

Some of the trees are 400 years old, and pollarding has recently been reintroduced. Young trees are cut through the trunk at about two metres from the ground so that there can be new growth safe from browsing deer. The sprouting branches provide fencing

INFORMATION

Distance: 7km
(4 1/2 miles).

Start and finish:
Lord Mayor's Drive
car park at the end of
Beeches Road,
Farnham Common.

Terrain: Roads,
tracks and good paths.
No special footwear
needed.

Refreshments: Car
park tea hut. Pubs at
Littleworth Common.

Public Transport:
Bus from Slough.

Burnham Beeches,
Mendelssohn's Path.

and firewood, while the stumpy tree is able to withstand strong winds and thus live longer.

Beyond the first crosspath the track is high up in woods above Mendelssohn's Slope. This path is sometimes known as Mendelssohn's Path after the composer, who used to walk here in the 1830s and 1840s whilst staying nearby. To the left in the trees can be seen a cattle fence. British White cattle, rare Berkshire pigs and Exmoor ponies are grazing as part of a policy of returning to traditional forest management.

Keep ahead until the path is running alongside this fence. At a junction bear right. (If the fence ends, you have gone a few metres too far.) This new path soon swings left and after a junction runs downhill into a valley. Cross the valley floor path - known as Victoria Drive - and climb up the other side. Where the path divides, take the left fork and go left again. After a few yards turn right into a gap in the trees to find an open grassed area. This is Pumpkin Hill Common. Keep forward with a road sometimes visible over to the left. The path runs straight ahead to meet a four-way road junction on the edge of Burnham Beeches. Cross the road and go to the right of the entrance to Juniper Hill to find a stile set back by a gate.

Go over the stile into a field. Walk ahead, keeping by the side of the field as the way runs downhill. As the path rises there is a view over to the left of Dorney Wood, the Chancellor of the Exchequer's official country residence, where pre-Budget meetings are occasionally held. The house dates from the 1920s.

At the far end of the field, go over the stiles at a road to continue westwards. As soon as the way becomes an enclosed track, go right over a stile to follow a field boundary northwards. The path soon curves before continuing north and passing a good example of a pollarded oak. There's another stile before the path runs up through a gap. The exit is ahead but the path runs to the right round the field to reach the stile at a road.

Go left along the road, which soon bears right to reach the Beech Tree at Littleworth Common. Turn down Common Lane opposite the pub. After the houses end on the right there is woodland on both sides. Go over the stile by the gate on the right. This is just a few yards before the Blackwood Arms - a charming free house noted for its choice of real ales from small independent brewers.

From the stile, the path leads to a second stile. Keep ahead down the side of the field, which later gently falls to two stiles in the field corner. Bear half-right down the next field to a kissing gate on the edge of Dorney Wood - the trees which have given their name to the Chancellor's nearby house. Keep straight ahead on the path which runs between the oaks and beeches - although not part of the Corporation of London-owned land, this is also 'Burnham Beeches'.

On the far side, go over a stile and cross a road to enter the City's Burnham Beeches. The path ahead is no longer open to traffic and nature has almost buried the metalled surface. At a junction the path is hard up against Hardicanute's 12th-century homestead moat on the left. For a clear view of the former defences, go round to the left and after a few yards turn left off the road.

Lord Mayors Drive.

The walk continues ahead down Halse Drive, where traffic is allowed although 'sleeping policemen' prevent any speeding - and there is a gate which can be closed. Stay on this road, which runs down into the valley and up to the junction where the walk started. Turn left to pass the tea hut and reach Beeches Road at Farnham Common.

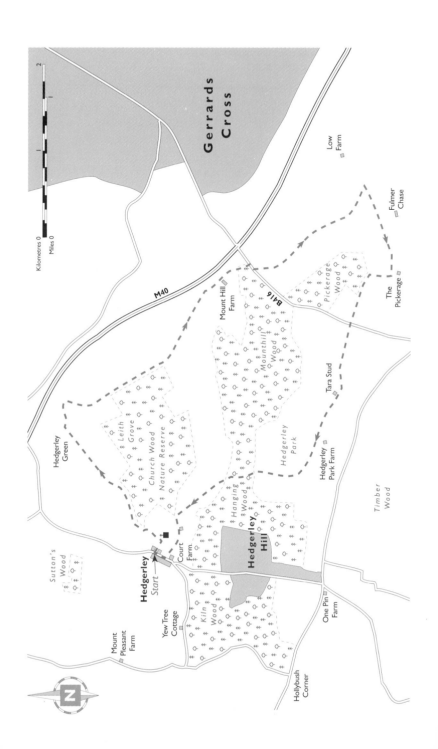

HEDGERLEY

Hedgerley, a southerly village but still within the Chiltern Hundreds, often wins the Best Kept Village in Buckinghamshire competition. This walk explores the surrounding countryside of the village, well known in the 12th and 13th centuries for its brickmaking. This is recalled by the Brickmould pub on the corner of Kiln Lane. The White Horse has been an inn since 1753 and still serves beer by gravity straight from the barrel.

Walk through the gates next to the White Horse to follow a short path up to the church. At the top of the slope there is a view over a pond and across the sloping Church Meadow. The present church was built in 1852, but framed inside is a fragment of Charles I's cloak, which he threw over the altar in the medieval church which was here until 1770. The King was displeased to find the altar bare and so donated his cloak as an instant altar cloth.

Continue up the wide path, which bends to give a view down on to the Old Rectory, dating from 1846 and now home to writer Lucinda Lambton who, with

INFORMATION

Distance: 7km (4 1/2 miles).

Start and finish: The White Horse at Hedgerley.

Terrain: Roads and paths. No special footwear needed.

Refreshments: The White Horse and The Brickmould at Hedgerley.

Public transport: Bus from Slough.

Hedgerley Green. Barn built with materials from old church.

her husband Sir Peregrine Worsthorne, added a gothic conservatory in 1994. At the top of the hill the path runs just inside a wood to reach Hedgerley Green where the ponds are believed to be the remains of the moat of Moat Farm - now cut off by the M4. The white building on the right is constructed out of materials from the old Hedgerley Church.

Leith Grove.

At the junction by the post box and Bulstrode Cottages, go right to pass Willow Tree Barn. Follow the lane round the bend and just before Manor Farm Cottage go right to find a footpath. The tree-fringed way soon narrows to run between fields. Later it is along the edge of Leith Grove woodland, which in spring is a mass of bluebells. Banks and ditches indicate that this is an old route. Beyond the wood the enclosed path runs down to a stile.

At once go over a second stile on the left and bear half-right along the side of a field. Ahead is the M4 motorway. The trees soon give way to a hedge. At the far end, go over a stile and ahead along a track. Beyond another stile by a gate the way is metalled to reach a main road at Dukes Valley.

Go right for a short distance before turning left behind the Fulmer Valley Farm sign into a footpath entrance. The way rises to turn the corner and run between paddocks and an orchard. Keep forward alongside a lake and where the water ends stay close to the fence to find the path still continuing ahead, beyond a stile, as an enclosed tunnel of trees.

At the far end, near a lake to the left, go over the stile and at once turn right for a few yards. Cross a ditch and go over a stile into a field. Turn left to go up the side of the field following the wood to the left. At the top go over a stile to a rising enclosed way.

Ahead can be seen a group of houses known as The Pickerage. Here the path crosses a working sandpit, so care should be taken in case there are vehicles crossing. The path turns right to pass an oak tree and after 100 metres bears left by the edge of Pickerage Wood to run directly to a stile at a road.

Go right to pass a bus stop and, before the cemetery, turn left over a stile into a field. Keep ahead along the side of the field. There are sometimes horned Highland cattle here. Despite their fierce appearance, they are gentle beasts. At the far end go over a stile and along a wooded path beside Tara Stud. At a junction go up steps ahead over a stile.

Bear over to the right to walk down to another stile, then head for a stile below the cedar tree. Go over a track and along the back of the end building to find a final stile. Walk half-right across a field to a stile in the corner by trees. A wide grass way bears round to the right. After a short distance go over a stile on the right and through a corner of the wood to cross a footbridge. Follow the path ahead alongside a field.

Hedgerley Church

Once inside Hanging Wood go over a stile and follow the path down through the trees. At the bottom a stile leads to a large field. On the far side is the Royal Society for the Protection of Birds' Church Wood Nature Reserve. This remnant of Chiltern woodland including beech, which once covered a much larger area, is a haven for the three woodpeckers - great spotted, green and lesser spotted - and the white admiral butterfly. Bear half left to the far corner where, in winter, Hedgerley Church can be seen on the hill.

In the field corner, go over a stile by a gate to follow a track to the pond in Village Lane in the centre of Hedgerley. Court Farm to the left was once the Church of England's Waifs and Strays Society 'Farm Home'. Turn right past the pond to reach The White Horse.

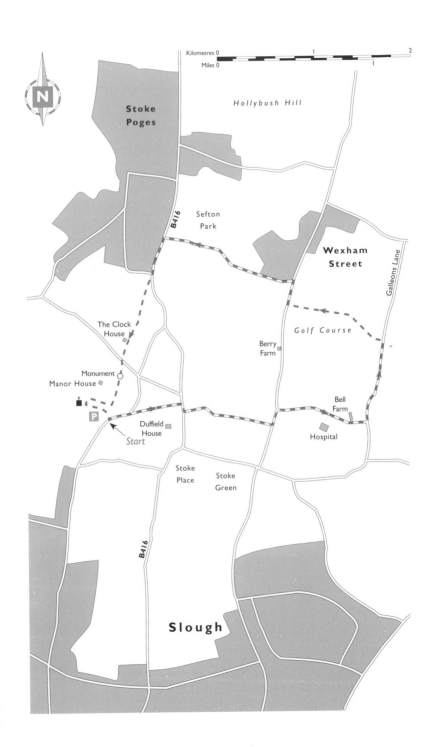

STOKE POGES

*E*legy Written in a Country Churchyard by Thomas Gray (1716-71) has been described as the most famous poem in the English language. Its author composed the final version at Stoke Poges, where he spent much time at his mother's house Stoke Court a mile to the north. His earlier work *Ode to the Spring* recalls the sights and sounds of the Buckinghamshire countryside. He loved walking alone, using the lanes and footpaths. This walk explores this countryside known to Gray and returns across Gray's Field with his monument and the church as the climax of the circular route. The church's location far from the village is due to the original Saxon decision to build by the manor house.

From the road entrance to Stoke Poges Church, walk north on the pavement. The church entrance is to the left and the car park to the right. On reaching Gray's Field entrance, cross the road and go up to a kissing

INFORMATION

Distance: 6km (4 miles).

Start and finish: Stoke Poges Church car park

Terrain: Roads and paths. Boots or strong footwear only needed in wet conditions.

Refreshments: The Plough in Wexham Street. Wide choice in nearby Slough.

Public Transport: Bus from Slough Station.

Yew at Stoke Poges Church.

gate half hidden behind an oak tree. Turn left to go through the gate and follow the path ahead which runs past several houses as the road swings away to the left. There are a couple more gates before the path becomes a road and meets a main road.

Cross over and turn right for a few metres before turning left up the wide entrance to Snitterfield House and farm. At the sharp bend, where the way divides to the house and farm, go to the right over grass to a stile.

A path runs ahead down a field to a second stile. Go forward up into a large field to see a tall chimney in the distance. Follow the field boundary on the right to the corner and go over a stile. Head across the next field to a stile by a road. Opposite is Wexham Park Hospital.

Turn left along the pavement, and when just beyond the hospital, cross the road to Bell Farm. There is a stile at the side of the gates. Follow the concrete farm road, with the hospital just visible to the right and a golf course to the left. Beyond a new house, Greenacres, the drive passes the main farm buildings including the farmhouse. After a short distance there is a gate and stile at the junction with a bridleway known as Gallions Lane.

Turn left and follow the well protected track north for 700 metres until a path joins from the left. Here turn left over a plank footbridge to Wexham Park Golf Course. Watch for flying balls before striking ahead over grass. Soon a path swings in from the left to also run towards the clubhouse. The way is over the car park and close to the golf clubhouse. Do not be tempted up the metalled driveway entrance, but keep on the grass over to its right to find a stile leading to a row of houses. Continue to a road and go right.

Ahead is Wexham Street. Turn left up Plough Lane to pass between the Old Cottage and The Plough inn. Follow the road round the corner where there are houses only to the right. At the sharp bend, leave the road by going ahead on to a bridleway. After a short distance the track meets Farthing Green Lane. Go ahead over a stile to follow an old tree-lined path between fields used by nearby stables.

Soon the way veers half-left up on to grass to reach kissing gates on each side of an old driveway to Sefton Park. Continue forward over grass with a view of the Georgian Sefton Park house, on the edge of Stoke Poges village, seen to the right. Beyond a large oak tree, the path meets a kissing gate by a bus stop on Bells Hill main road. Cross over and turn left to walk to the end of the houses by Rogers Lane.

Go through the kissing gate on the corner and follow the path across to another kissing gate. Go half-right to cut across the corner of the next field to yet another kissing gate and then half left over a stream to a gap in the field boundary. Keep to the right side of the field and on into the next field to pass close to a house on the right. At the far end cross a road to enter Gray's Field.

Gray monument.

Bear half left towards the massive monument which was erected in 1799 in memory of Thomas Gray. The design is by architect James Wyatt and the positioning of the dramatic monument away from the churchyard is said to have beeen determined by the landscape gardener Humphrey Repton. Over to the right there is a glimpse of the church and the Manor House with its tall chimneys dating from Elizabeth I's reign.

Turn right down the short end of the field to find a kissing gate leading into the outer churchyard. Turn right through the lychgate for the church which has Saxon, Norman, early Gothic and Tudor work. Gray is buried outside the east end in a family tomb which had no room for his name. Outside the porch is the yew where The Elegy was written in 1750. Inside the west end of the church is the mysterious 'Bicycle Window' showing a figure on an early form of scooter.

View of monument through the Stoke Poges lychgate.

Turn left at the lychgate to follow a path to the road. The car park is across the road to the right.

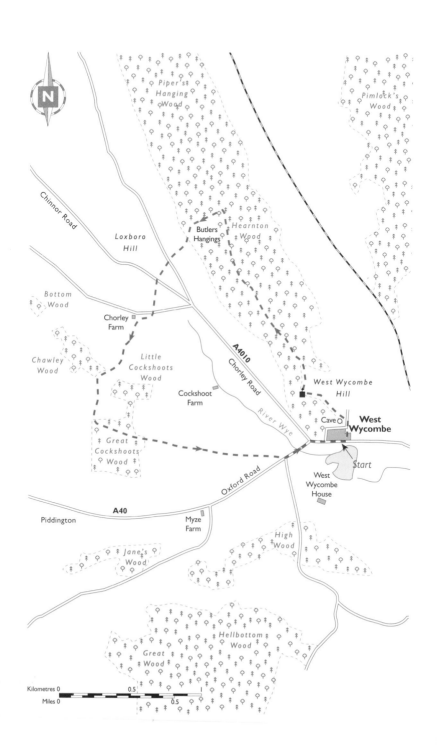

WEST WYCOMBE

W est Wycombe is in the care of the National Trust but the figure dominating the village is Sir Francis Dashwood, the 18th-century founder of the exclusive and notorious Hellfire Club. Dashwood, who also had the title Baron Le Despencer, was Chancellor of the Exchequer in 1761-62 and Postmaster-General from 1766 to 1781, in which year he died. As well as the Hellfire Club he founded the Knights of St Francis of Wycombe, equally notorious for their sacreligious activities.

This walk goes up two hills to find good views over the unique Chiltern village where only two houses have been built this century. The oldest building in the principally 18th-century main street is the Church Room and Loft, open for teas on summer Sundays, which was built in the 15th century for Bisham

Worn Pilgrim Stone.

INFORMATION

Distance: 6km (3 1/2 miles).

Start and finish: The Loft, next to the newsagents, in West Wycombe main street.

Terrain: Roads, tracks and paths. No special footwear needed.

Refreshments: Pubs in West Wycombe. The Loft for teas on summer Sundays. Café at Caves.

Public Transport: Train to High Wycombe then bus.

Opening hours: West Wycombe Caves: Daily Mar-Oct and winter weekends, 1100-1700. Admission charge. West Wycombe House: Jun-Aug, Sun-Thu 1400-1800. Admission charge. Grounds also open Apr-May.

Abbey. Outside is a stone where pilgrims to St Frideswide's shrine near Oxford knelt to kiss a crucifix which remained here until destroyed by the Roundheads.

Go under Church Loft, next to the newsagents, to walk up Church Lane. Immediately to the right is a furniture-making factory. Continue up the hill past the cottages.

Only take the path and road to the left if you wish to visit the caves and café. The caves were extended to a depth of 400 metres in the 1750s by Sir Francis who wanted to provide local employment. The spoil was used for making the straight road into High Wycombe and the caves were used for meetings of the Hellfire Club, which also met at Medmenham (Walk 7). Today visitors to the Hellfire Caves see life-size figures of Dashwood and some of its thirteen members, such as Lord Sandwich and reformer John Wilkes, who were rumoured to be involved in strange rituals and abandoned behaviour.

The walk continues ahead at the junction but after a short distance go left, opposite a gateway, on to a path which soon runs up to barriers. The way is then uphill over grass towards the right side of the monument on top of Church Hill to enter the churchyard. Here look back for the view to High Wycombe up the straight main road.

The open air six-sided mausoleum was erected by Dashwood in 1765. Besides his family monuments there is one to Paul Whitehead, the Hellfire Club steward, whose heart was placed here amid firing of cannons at the end of a two-hour funeral ceremony.

The path runs through the main churchyard to the west door of the church which stands on an iron age fort. The old church was given its Georgian appearance by Sir Francis who placed the golden ball on top of the 14th-century tower after being inspired during a visit to Venice. There is room for six people to sit inside the ball which led John Wilkes to call it

View of West Wycombe
House and village from
church.

"the best Globe Tavern I was ever in" after Dashwood
entertained him there to "divine milk punch, and jolly
songs very unfit for the profane ears below".

Leave the church door by turning right to a gate and
walking over the parking area with views on both
sides. On this hilltop, until plague struck in the 18th
century, there was a village called Haveringham.
Follow the lane round to the right but just before a
gate turn sharp left on to a bridleway. The track runs
north through scrub and woodland with good views of
the Chiltern hills to the west.

Later there is a field on the right. Where the main
track divides keep to the right. Soon the field gives
way to Hearnton Wood. At a clear four-way junction
go left. There is some new planting before the path
drops down between beech trees to a gate at the
bottom of the slope.

Here you have a good view of the countryside 60m below in the valley. Bear half-left downhill on the chalk downland and through the scrub known as Butlers Hangings. Found in the grassland are two Chiltern specialities - the wild candytuft and Chiltern gentian. The area is also noted for its huge number of spiders, including the purse web spider.

At a gate, follow the hedge down to stiles at a lane. The path goes half-left across the next field to another lane crossing flanked by stiles. On the far side there is a view down on to a farm with the golden ball of West Wyvombe church seen up to the left. Walk down the field to a stile by a gate opposite Chorley Farm. Its timber-framed farmhouse dates from Charles I's reign.

Go up the lane at the side of the farm. The way double-bends round the back of the farmhouse and gently climbs the hill. In the fields each side dairy herds have given way to crops in recent years. Partridges and pheasants are likely to be seen here.

Lake at West Wycombe.

At a path junction in the wood, go left up a track which bends to run alongside a field. This lane is believed to be part of a longer pre-Roman route. At a junction, keep ahead for a few metres looking for a steep footpath entrance on the left. Go up the slope into Great Cockshoots Wood, where there is a waymark on a tree. The way through the trees and over a crosstrack is well waymarked with with arrows on the larch and beech trees. On the far side a stile leads on to open field.

Keep forward as the trees on the right give way to a hedge. There is a view of the church on the hill. At a gap the path passes into another field where there is a view of West Wycombe House dating from the time of the famous Sir Francis, who dammed the River Wye and staged mock naval battles on the lake. At a hawthorn tree, go into a third field to continue downhill to a squeeze stile by the road.

Go left along the path by the road to pass the cattle pound just before a road junction. Keep ahead to walk up the main street, passing The George & Dragon with its 18th-century sign to reach The Loft.

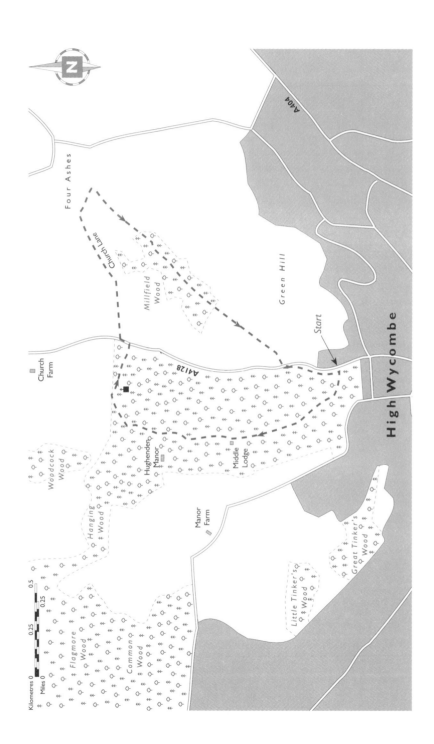

WALK 13

HUGHENDEN

The memory of Benjamin Disraeli has prevented High Wycombe from spreading northwards into the Hughenden Manor parkland which preserves the timeless setting of the parish church, where sheep wander in the churchyard, and the Victorian premier's country home on the hill.

Hughenden Manor.

INFORMATION

Distance: 4km (2 1/2 miles).

Start and finish: Hughenden Park car park, Hughenden Road (A4128).

Terrain: Paths and grass. No special footwear needed except in wet weather.

Refreshments: Tearoom at Hughenden Manor stable yard open Wed-Sun afternoons. Teas served at Church House in churchyard on summer Sundays and August weekends.

Public transport: Rail to High Wycombe then bus.

Opening hours: *Hughenden Manor:* Mar: Sat-Sun 1400-1800. Apr-Sept: Wed-Sat 1400-1800, Sun 1200-1800. Oct: Wed-Sat: 1400-17-00, Sun 1200-1700. Admission charge to house (National Trust members free).

Hughenden was a Georgian building when Disraeli purchased it in 1848. The gothic appearance is the work of architect E.B. Lamb in the 1860s. The house, in the care of the National Trust, is packed with the Prime Minister's intimate effects including manuscripts of his novels and labels sent with primroses by Queen Victoria. The study is much as he left it at his death in 1881 and as seen by the Queen who spent time in the room a few days after his funeral. He was PM from 1874 to 1880 and during this time was given the title 1st Earl of Beaconsfield.

The walk starts as soon as the houses in Hughenden Road give way to countryside. From the lodge at the southern end of the park, follow the metalled path to a bridge. Here the hard surface ends as the way bears round to the right to run gently uphill with the stream down to the right. This was once the main driveway used by visitors, including Queen Victoria, who drove here from High Wycombe Station. The stream was "the Ancient River" to Disraeli.

Soon there is a brief glimpse over to the left of the top of a monument commemorating Disraeli's father, the son of an Italian-Jewish immigrant. The column was erected secretly in 1862 under the direction of Disraeli's wife as a surprise for her husband who first saw it on returning home after a long absence.

On reaching a gateway at a second lodge, skirt its garden by going round to the right to find a stile before continuing north up the path. Down to the right can be seen a lake and half left is the house and garden. At the double gates, bear round to the right to cross a stile and continue along the top of the valley. After a view up to the side of the manor house there is the cream Old Vicarage. The path meets the main driveway at a cattle grid.

Disraeli's Tomb at Hughenden churchyard.

To visit the house, shop or tearoom go left. The walk continues to the right down the metalled driveway to pass the church which, although old, is very much a shrine to Disraeli who is buried outside the west end. The tomb includes the name of Mrs Brydges Willyams, a widow from Torquay, who was rewarded with the promise of burial in the family vault for having helped Disraeli through a financial crisis. Inside in the chancel is a generously worded monument placed there by Queen Victoria. The Garter banner once hung in St George's Chapel at Windsor. At the back of the church is a key with a circle in the handle which was used as a temporary ring by poor couples at weddings.

Continue beyond the church to go through a gate and across a bridge. The chalk stream is fed by a spring a few yards upstream, so even in drought this water flows strongly. At the lodge go left along the road for a short distance to cross Valley Road and go up a signposted bridleway running up the side of the valley.

The path, known locally as Church Lane, is at first fenced at the side of a field before bearing off half-left as a sunken track lined by trees. At a junction at the top, go right over a stile by a farm gate and pass in front of a house called Millfield to another stile by a gate. Bear half-right down the field towards the wood ahead. At a gap, pass into another field and follow the wood on the right to the next field corner. Here go half-right on to a woodland path where there is a notice announcing Millfield Wood.

This woodland was owned by Disraeli, who loved trees and could see the wood from his library window. The beech trees were intended for the High Wycombe chair industry but also found here are ash and cherry. In spring there is a lovely haze of bluebells.

Follow the path through the trees, with a brief glimpse of Hughenden Church below. On emerging from the wood, go right with the trees down the side of the field. Before the bottom, the path goes through a gap on the right. Once in the next field, go left downhill to steps leading the road. Cross over with care to go over a bank and find a metalled path. Turn left to walk downhill to the lodge at the start of the walk.

Lodge at Hughenden.

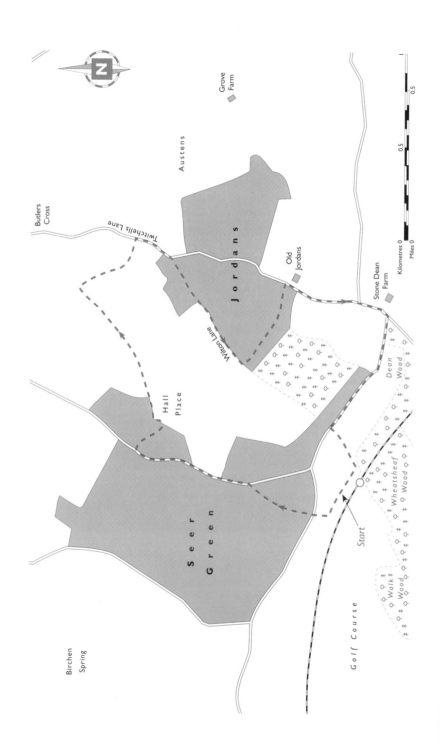

Grove Farm

Austens

Butlers Cross

Twitchells Lane

Jordans

Old Jordans

Stone Dean Farm

Wilton Lane

Hall Place

Dean Wood

Seer Green

Wheatsheaf Wood

Walk Wood

Start

Birchen Spring

Golf Course

Kilometres 0   0.5   1
Miles 0   0.5

SEER GREEN AND JORDANS

J ordans is a model village built by Quakers alongside Old Jordans, which has a special place in Quaker history. This walk passes through Seer Green with its Victorian church to the early 20th-century village which has an attractive new green but a much older place of worship.

The station, until recently known as Seer Green & Jordans Halt, has substantial rooms thanks to funding by Jordans. Take the footpath which starts at the far side of the car park opposite the platform entrance. The way is behind a fence and alongside the trees to go into a wood. The metalled path turns right sharply downhill to cross a road.

The now enclosed path rises to cross a residential road. Through the trees on the left is a glimpse of the Old Vicarage and its gothic porch dating from about 1850. The path joins Vicarage Close at a road still called School Lane. Turn left here to pass Seer Green School.

Beyond the parish hall and Fair View, School Lane becomes Chalfont Lane, leading to Seer's triangular green, which since 1845 has been occupied by the parish church. By tradition, the gate near The Three Horsehoes is used for funerals and the one by The Jolly Cricketers for weddings.

Continue past the the church and post office to a crossroads by a garage. Turn right into Hearnes Meadow. Once round the bend, keep to the left of the small green to find a path running between houses to fields. At the footpath junction, go left to follow the fenced footpath which has a double bend.

INFORMATION

Distance: 6km (4 miles).

Start and finish: Seer Green & Jordans Station.

Terrain: Metalled paths and one sometimes muddy path. No special footwear needed.

Refreshments: Pubs at Seer Green; Old Jordans serves lunches and teas.

House on the Green at Jordans.

At a stile the way continues north, but just inside a playing field. At the far end there is a set-back stile leading to a field. Stay by the field boundary on the right and where it falls away keep ahead. On leaving the field there is a crosspath. Go right to cross a stile. Follow the path left for a few metres before going ahead, along the side of the field and under the power cables.

Just before the end of the path, bear left over grass to a stile. Turn left along a rough lane, which has a concrete surface when it descends to Twitchells Lane. Turn right to pass the Jordans village sign. Stay on the right of the road to bear right at a junction into Wilton Lane. The metalled surface ends as the lane narrows to continue as a bridleway. Where the path narrows again, there are barriers to the right to prevent horses from taking a path to Seer Green. Here go left, uphill, to the edge of Crutches Wood, which lost most of its beeches in the 1987 Great Storm. Go over the crossroads, keeping the wood on the right, to reach The Green at Jordans.

This is a model Quaker village with cottages built between 1919 and 1923 under the direction of architect Fred Rowntree. The little building on the green is the estate office. The thriving Village Store has won best post office and best stores awards. Cricket was played on the green until a celebrated 1994 court action over balls landing in a garden led to a move south to Chalky Fields to maintain good relations.

Continue ahead passing more cottages, each with its own name such as Candlemas on the right and

Jordans Meeting House.

Shepherd Cottage on the left at the junction with Jordans Lane. Cross the road to the entrance of Jordans Farm and turn right on a footpath which runs behind the hedge. At the end, return to the road to pass Old Jordans.

In the 17th century, Old Jordans was a farmhouse where George Fox and William Penn attended secret meetings of the Society of Friends (the Quakers). The building is now a Quaker guest house and conference centre open to all.

Penn had a turbulent life. Three times imprisoned for his beliefs (which attacked the religious doctrine of the day), he never wavered in his principles, and in 1686 managed to secure the release of nearly 2000 people imprisoned for religious reasons. The American state of Pennsylvania, which he founded in 1682, is actually named for his father, Admiral Sir William Penn.

The dining room, where Friends met illegally, has a door said to have come from the *Mayflower* which took the Pilgrim Fathers to America. The barn, built in the year the ship was broken up, is reputed to contain Mayflower timber. In recent times, the composer Benjamin Britten and and the tenor Peter Pears were among those who came to perform inside with local

Barn and Old Jordans.

musicians. The garden may be viewed, and visitors can walk through the gate beyond the barn and follow a path down through the orchard to a kissing gate to reach the Meeting House. Those continuing on the road should walk on the right.

The Meeting House was built by Quakers in 1688, as soon as the Declaration of Indulgence ended the persecution of non-conformists. Among those buried outside is William Penn, who stayed at Stone Dean just south of Welders Lane.

Continue beyond the Meeting House and Welders Lane. At the next road junction go right into Long Bottom Lane. After just over 1km turn left into Farm Lane. Keep right at a fork to reach Seer Green & Jordans Station.

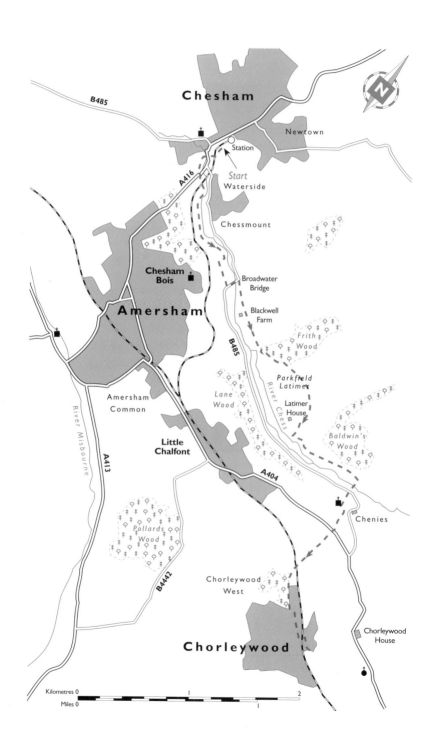

THE CHESS VALLEY

Chesham Station is at the end of a Metropolitan branch line opened in 1889. The River Chess rises at Chesham which means 'water meadow by a pile of stones' and this walk, between Underground stations, follows part of the Chess Valley Walk before striking uphill to the village of Chenies with its Tudor manor.

From Chesham Station, follow the enclosed path which passes a fine water tower for the steam engines which once ran out of here to Baker Street. Do not be tempted over the railway line but continue downhill to bear right down a short road to a Baptist church by the main road. Cross the road to enter Meades Water Gardens.

Turn left along the bank of the River Chess, which soon narrows before being forced through a fast run. Keep ahead to return to the road. Cross over at the junction to walk down Moor Road. Soon there is a pavement on the left by the river. Pass under the railway line and keep on the pavement, which becomes a riverside path as the road swings away.

Here the river is wide with islands and swans can often be seen. Do not cross the bridge to Christ Church Waterside but go right to the road and then left past the houses. At the T-junction, keep ahead by the phone box to cross a stream to a playing field. Bear left to find the river again and follow the bank towards a leaning tree. A path runs through the woods and for a time there is water on both sides.

River Chess below Latimer House.

On coming to a waterfall at a path junction, continue ahead on the opposite bank. At a footbridge, cross the water to follow a narrow enclosed path which double-bends round a Chiltern spring water bottling plant on the site of Chess watercress beds.

INFORMATION

Distance: 12km (7 miles).

Start: Chesham Station.

Finish: Chorleywood Station.

Terrain: Roads, tracks and paths. Parts of the walk can be muddy, so strong footwear is advised.

Refreshments: Mill Farm shop at Chenies Bottom sells ice cream; The Bedford Arms at Chenies and The Sportsman opposite Chorleywood Station.

Opening hours: Chenies Manor House: Apr-Oct, Wed-Thu 1400-1700; Admission charge

A kissing gate leads into a field. Go left at a gateway ahead go over the stile and along a track to a road. Keep forward at a junction and turn left. Follow the main road (walking on the right side) to cross the River Chess at Broadwater Bridge and, as the road bends left, go ahead to the start of a track. Here go over the stile on the right.

Keep ahead along the edge of the sloping field with the river below. After a double bend bear slightly left, keeping a chestnut tree to the right. The path runs gently uphill to a stile before beginning to go downhill. Beyond a gate with a stile, the way is by a high wall. At a cottage, go right to a road at a double bend. Turn left and keep forward on a track as the road bears left.

To the right is timber-framed Blackwell Farm. Keep forward and to the left of a dividing hedge. Go over a stile by a gate and keep by the hedge on the right through three fields. At the far end take the path along the edge of the wood. The way climbs, giving views down on to the river, and at the top cuts through the wood to a large field. Keep to the right to reach a couple of stiles leading on to a road by Parkfield Latimer.

Turn right along the road which soon runs downhill to Latimer. On the left is the Old Rectory. As a young man, the architect Sir George Gilbert Scott stayed here with his uncle. Following his great successes with the Albert Memorial and St Pancras Station in London, he was asked to enlarge the church here in 1867. Beyond the church to the right is Latimer House, former home of Lord Chesham and now Coopers & Lybrand conference centre.

Go left past Latimer Cottage, once the butler's residence, to the second gate on the left. Here the path swings left to a kissing gate. Continue over a field to another kissing gate and down between high hedges to emerge by Latimer village green. The heart and harness of a horse which served in the Boer War are buried beneath the stone near the war memorial.

At the parish pump, go right, and where the houses end go over a stile on the left. Cross a second stile and bear half-left to continue along the valley. The high path gives a good view down on to the river which here once had watercress beds. In the wood below are traces of Flaunden's 13th-century church, succeeded in 1838 by the one in the new village 2km to the north.

Beyond a stile and gate is the lonely tomb (guarded by two trees) of William Liberty, a member of the family later associated with Liberty's store, who died in 1777. Beyond another gate the path runs above a braid of the Chess before passing through Mill Farm farmyard at Chenies Bottom. Turn right over the bridge, and after a second bend the road passes the former mill on the main river.

Weather vane at Mill Farm.

Where the road divides, go right up to the main road and cross over to enter a wood. Take the less well defined left-hand path up through the trees to the corner of the wood at the top of the hill. An enclosed path runs between high walls to pass Chenies Manor and Church.

The Manor House was built about 1460 for Sir John Cheyne. Henry VIII, visiting when it was the home of the first Earl of Bedford, was much taken with the twisting chimneys, which were copied for Hampton Court.

Turn left to follow the wide drive down to the village green laid out by the Duke of Bedford in the 19th century. Go right to follow the road round a bend and along to the white Claypit Cottages at the main road. Cross straight over to continue ahead down a rough hedged lane.

River Chess at Chenies Bottom.

At the bottom of the hill, the track runs through Halsey's Wood and under the Metropolitan Line. On the far side, leave the main path by bearing left on to a 'no horses' path running through the young beech trees. Later the way follows a line of back gardens. At the far end, turn left down to a residential road. Go right to reach shops, and at Shire Lane crossroads, go left under the bridge and right up to Chorleywood Station.

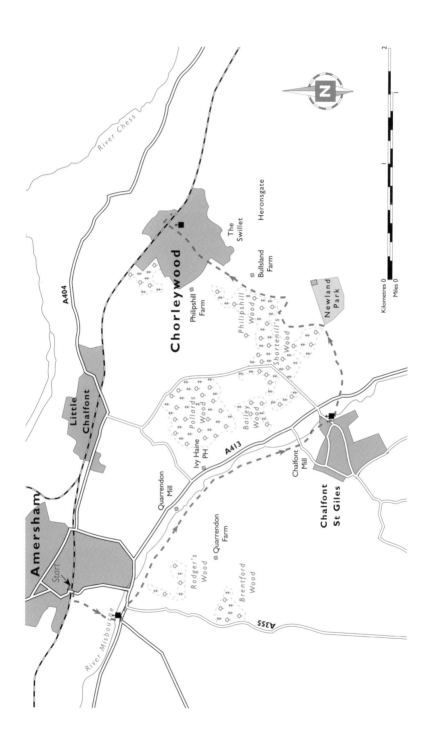

AMERSHAM TO CHORLEYWOOD

This walk between two counties and two stations makes use of the Metropolitan Line which was promoted as the 'Line of Health' when run by the Great Central Railway. The tiny River Misbourne, which has an erractic flow from its source at Great Missenden, is the recurring feature along the valley between Amersham and Chalfont St Giles before the walk goes over high ground, where a new village of rescued Chiltern buildings can be found, to follow an ancient lane along the Buckinghamshire-Hertfordshire boundary.

Turn left out of Amersham Station and go left again under the railway bridge. At once cross the road to go right up a metalled path (easily missed, so be sure to find it) below the railway embankment. On reaching another road, go left for a few metres before following a path into the wood. The way, parallel with the road, later widens before running downhill. Ignore all turnings and soon the path is metalled as it leaves the wood. Below in the valley is Old Amersham.

Continue downhill and at a junction bear left and then right over the River Misbourne to reach the churchyard. Amersham Church is partly 12th-century with plenty of memorials to the Drake family of Shardeloes (see Walk 17). In 1682 a Drake built the nearby Market Hall which dominates the High Street. Every year on 19-20 September the road is closed for the annual fun fair marking the parish patronal festival. The 16th-century interior of the Crown inn featured in the film *Four Weddings and a Funeral*.

At the High Street, with the Market Hall on the right, turn left to pass the Griffin where Cromwell's troops were billeted. On the same side is number 60 which has a notice issued in 1811 by the magistrates of the Hundred warning against 'Common Beggars, Ballad Singers and other Vagrants'. Continue beyond the

INFORMATION

Distance: 12km (7 1/2 miles).

Start: Amersham Station.

Finish: Chorleywood Station.

Terrain: Road, track and path. Boots or strong footwear recommended.

Refreshments: Pubs and Tesco (cafe) at Old Amersham; Merlin's Cave pub and Tea Time teashop at Chalfont St Giles.

Opening hours: *John Milton's Cottage:* Mar-Oct: Wed-Sun 1000-1300; 1400-1800; admission charge.

Chiltern Open Air Museum: Apr-Oct: Wed-Sun 1400-1800; admission charge.

Public Transport: Underground (Metropolitan Line) and Chiltern Railways.

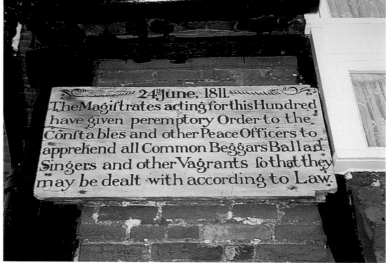

24ᵗʰ June, 1811. The Magistrates acting for this Hundred have given peremptory Order to the Constables and other Peace Officers to apprehend all Common Beggars Ballad Singers and other Vagrants so that they may be dealt with according to Law.

Top:
The King's Arms, Amersham.

Bottom:
Notice in Amersham.

roundabout by Fox's to Bury Farm on the right. At the side of Bury Cottage, go over the stile and bear round to the left.

Beyond a cattle grid the way is ahead over a field to go under the by-pass, where stiles and a fence guide walkers away from the often muddy surface in the tunnel. Once in the long field, keep ahead past a stile to the right. Over to the left is the Misbourne. Here in the field the path is parallel to, but away from, the hedge on the right. Head for a stile, not in the field corner but at the bottom of the field's slope.

After the stile, a path runs ahead along the side of a field. Soon after crossing a track from the Misbourne, the visible field boundary ends and the path becomes the boundary as it runs across open country. Over to the left is a mill on the Misbourne. Later the path is by a high hedge hiding waterworks. Go over the stile and soon another by a gate. When the hedge falls away there is a view to the (unreachable from here) Ivy House pub with its three gothic windows. Head across the large field towards a stile ahead - a few yards from the corner to the left. From the stile go half-right across a small field to a stile by a lane.

Cross the lane to a stile and keep ahead to a second stile. Still keep forward along the bottom of a slope to the trees ahead, keeping the pylon to the left. Go over a stile and follow the path ahead running through a long strip of woodland. On meeting a road at a double bend continue ahead past the Old Mill entrance and take the rough track ahead while the road swings left to ford the Misbourne.

After a line of new houses the way is enclosed before entering another strip of woodland. Soon the path joins a wide former driveway with some recent houses alongside. Ahead is the main street of Chalfont St Giles.

The village, which has a green, carefully tended pond and a line of little shops was the set for 'Warmington-on-Sea' in the *Dad's Army* film with The Crown becoming Captain Mainwaring's bank. John Milton came here in 1665 to escape the Great Plague in London and to complete *Paradise Lost*. His cottage and garden, in the main street, can be visited.

Cross the road and go right for a few yards to turn left under the archway next to the newsagents. Beyond the church gate, an enclosed path follows the churchyard round a double bend to a kissing gate. Go over the footbridge to cross the Misbourne and follow

Milton's Cottage,
Chalfont St Giles.

the clear path ahead over the meadow to another
kissing gate. Here a narrow fenced path runs up to the
main road. Cross over to take a hidden path between
The Edge and an unmarked driveway.

The narrow path runs uphill and along by back
gardens. At a divide go left over a stile. This path bears
round to a second stile. Keep forward as the hedge on
the left turns away. On the far side of the field, go over
a stile in the hedge to cross a smaller field with a view
of Ashwell's Farm to the right. Go over the two stiles
ahead and at once turn right to a stile in the corner of
a third field.

Cross the road to go round the barrier and follow the
long straight woodland path for just over 400m to
meet another road opposite the entrance to Newland
Park. The late 18th-century house is now part of

Brunel University, with the Chiltern Open Air Museum in the grounds. The growing number of buildings saved from demolition by being moved here include a chair factory from High Wycombe, a toll-gate and a forge.

Go through the gateway and past the lodge to bear left to a stile leading to a field. Go ahead towards a tree to follow the left hand side of the huge field. The museum buildings are on the right. At the far end of the field, in the corner, go over a stile and follow a woodland path which soon runs downhill. Eventually the way meets a rough lane at a bend.

Turn left to follow the sunken lane as it runs gently uphill. This track is Old Shire Lane, marking the boundary between Buckinghamshire and Hertfordshire. At the top is the entrance to Philipshill Wood, now owned by the Woodland Trust. Here the lane widens and there is a view of Bullsland Farm across to the right. After Piggy Lane (right) the way is metalled with some houses. At the Heronsgate Road junction, on the edge of Chorleywood, the road becomes just Shire Lane with through traffic.

Keep ahead to pass the Orchard which was designed by architect Charles Voysey as his own home. At Haddon Road there is a rare Edward VIII post box, placed here in 1936 during the king's short reign. Continue ahead downhill to pass St John Fisher Church, which opened in 1955 and is partly a converted Voysey cottage. Go under the railway bridge and turn right to walk up to Chorleywood Station.

The fine Chorleywood Common, crisscrossed by bridleways and dominated by the church with its spire, lies just north of the station.

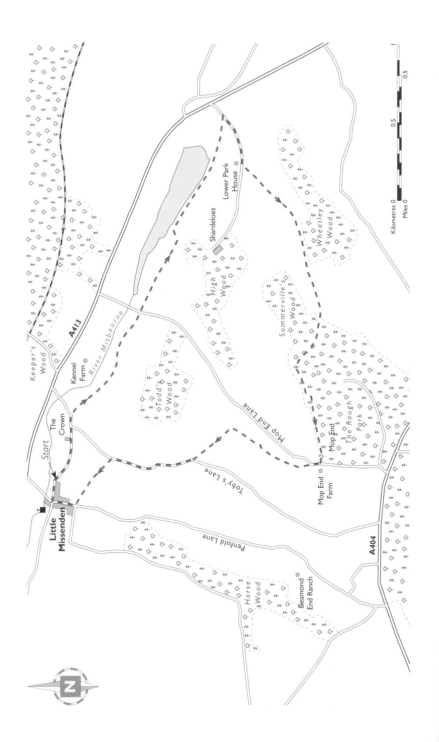

LITTLE MISSENDEN AND MOP END

L ittle Missenden is a sleepy village free of through traffic. This walk explores the Shardeloes estate nearby, returning by way of an ancient green lane with a view down to the village.

INFORMATION

Distance: 8km (5 miles).

Start and finish: The Red Lion on The Green at Little Missenden.

Terrain: Roads, track, grass and paths. Grass can be muddy in wet weather, in which case strong footwear is advised.

Refreshments: Pubs at Little Missenden.

Public transport: Bus from Amersham.

Little Missenden Church.

The church at Little Missenden dates from 975 with much of the Saxon and later Norman work remaining. The chancel arch includes Roman bricks. On entering the building, you see a huge 13th-century wall painting of St Christopher carrying the Christ Child across water. Alongside is the picture story of St Catherine. There is another mural in the Lady Chapel which has a large map of the parish. To the church's east side is the early 16th-century Manor House, once the home of Dr Bates, a member of the notorious Hell Fire Club at West Wycombe (Walk 12).

The walk starts on The Green outside the 18th-century Red Lion where there are a few tables at the back overlooking the River Misbourne and often

Cottages on the green at Little Missenden.

plenty of ducks. From The Green turn east, away from the church, to walk to the far end of the village. Soon there is the 18th-century Missenden House and, after 300 yards, The Crown which has been run by the same family since 1920.

As the road begins to bear left to the Mill End bridge over the River Misbourne, go ahead through a kissing gate waymarked South Bucks Way. Follow the farm track but keep ahead over a stile by (usually open) gates when the main track swings left to Kennel Farm. On reaching a fenced bridleway, Mop End Lane, cross the stile and go through the kissing gate to continue in the same easterly direction. Where the way divides, take the left fork to go over a double stile and enter the Lower Park of Shardeloes estate. The path runs to the left of the line of trees ahead and near the lake on the left.

Soon the mansion can be seen up on the hill to the right. Shardeloes, on the site of an earlier house known to Elizabeth I, was built between 1758 and 1766 for Amersham's then MP, William Drake. The design owes much to the last-minute employment of then unknown young Robert Adam, who revised the original plans. The house is now divided into several residences. The grounds were laid out by Repton, who made a feature of the lake fed by the River Misbourne which is boosted by springs just upstream of Little Missenden. Unfortunately today's erratic water flow means that the lake's splendid expanse of water, home to much waterfowl, has been known to dry up. In Victorian winters the residents of Amersham often came here to skate.

At the far end of the parkland, go over a stile and follow a short path to a kissing gate leading to a cricket ground. Bear half-left to pass the pavilion and reach the lodges at the main entrance to Shardeloes. Turn right to walk up the main metalled driveway. The way rises gently, giving a view up the valley. Just before drawing level with Lower Park House, go left through the second of two kissing gates. Follow a field boundary to the left on a path which runs gently down into the valley. At the bottom the path bears to the right to become a more substantial track and run alongside Wheatley Wood.

Keep ahead to eventually reach a double stile on the edge of a wood. There is a hide to the left of this conservation area owned by National Power, who have a well-screened sub-station in the trees. Beyond the stiles, bear round to the left to walk through the wood. There is a fence to left and then one to the right. The way is uphill and briefly in the open before running through more woodland. The path bears left to go under power lines and then right, back into woodland. The path passes below another pylon and later, shortly after barriers, reaches a lane at Mop End.

Shardeloes.

Turn right along the lane to pass Griffin Cottage to the entance to Mop End Farm. At the farm gateway, go over the stile on the right and walk half-left to the far end of the fence to the left. Go over the stile and turn sharp right to follow the hedge at the side of a huge field. Keep past the pylon to the gap at the far end. Here go half-left across a smaller field to another gap in a field corner. In the next field, go left to cut the corner and look for a stile on the left leading to Toby's Lane.

Turn right down the ancient hedged way which runs downhill. Just beyond Breaches Wood there is a view down to Little Missenden. After 200 m, go over the stile on the left and walk down the field, passing close to a solitary tree. At the bottom of the hill and in the corner of the field go over the stile by the gates. Ahead is Penfold Lane, but go right past Town Farm and Town Cottage to the T-junction opposite The Manor House. The church is to the left and The Green to the right.

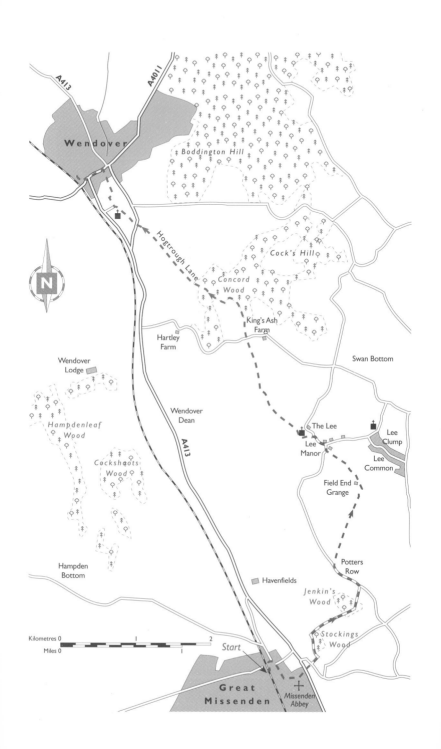

GREAT MISSENDEN TO WENDOVER

When the railway arrived at Great Missenden in 1892 one of the first commuters was Arthur Liberty, founder of Liberty's of Regent Street, who had his own marble seat at Marylebone Station. He had been born in Chesham, where his father ran a draper's, and was deeply attached to the Chiltern countryside.

This walk linking two Chiltern Line stations passes through The Lee, an attractive village with a green, where the successful Sir Arthur bought the manor house and imposed good taste on the pub and church. Wendover is reached by way of a woodland track.

INFORMATION

Distance: 10km (6 miles).

Start: Great Missenden Station.

Finish: Wendover Station.

Terrain: Roads, tracks and paths. Strong footwear needed in wet conditions.

Refreshments: Pubs in Great Missenden, The Lee and Wendover. Le Petit Cafe teashop in Pound Street Wendover as well as several pubs.

Tourist Information: Wendover Clock Tower, Mon-Sat 1000-1600.

Stocking's Wood.

Turn left out of Great Missenden Station to walk down past shops to a T-junction. Turn right along the High Street to pass The Keys and at The George, go left into Church Street. After a bend the Abbey Farmhouse is on the right with a glimpse of the battlements of the late 18th-century gothic Missenden Abbey, which stands on the site of a monastery founded in 1133.

The lane to the right, as indicated by the notice on the tree, leads up over the by-pass to the church. But the walk continues ahead to the tunnel running under the by-pass, through trees and under another road to run steeply up to a lane. Go left to walk towards two gateways including the entrance to Frith Hill Stables. Keep between the two to find a small gate leading to a narrow path. Beyond a stile is Stocking's Wood, an ancient woodland where wood-sorrel and primroses are found. Keep ahead and when the path has passed a crater to the right, and is above a field to the left, the way is downhill. Go over a stile at a path junction and go right over another stile.

The way is uphill with trees to the left at first to reach a stile at the top. Follow the fence to the right and, just before reaching the field's narrow corner, cut the corner to go over a stile into Jenkin's Wood. This carefully managed wood, where there has been recent felling, contains some earthworks indicating a 12th-century manorial site. The perimeter is sometimes known as the 'Nun's Walk'. A path runs half-left through the small wood to a stile where there is a view of two white houses. Go half-left across a field to a stile by a gate at a road.

Turn left to follow the road through the scattered hamlet of Potters Row. Beyond a left turning to Park Hill is the Firs, which was built in 1861 for the painter William Callow, who taught Louis Philippe's family after the French king abdicated and escaped to England under the name of 'Mr Smith'. After a short distance go right at the side of Hedgesparrow Cottage where a stile and gateway under an oak leads into a

View from footpath near The Lee.

field. Keep ahead when the hedge falls away. Looking back to the left is a view of the former Lamb pub with its faded sign on the wall.

On the far side of the field, go over two stiles and bear half-right to a stile in the corner of the next field. Again go half-right to the far corner stile. Keep ahead across a field to go downhill and join another path by the hedge to the left. The way runs up to a stile by a gate where there is a handy seat. Continue ahead along the lane, which runs downhill past Field End Grange. At the crossroads, go ahead on a path which runs up a slope and double bends. After a third bend up, the track runs straight ahead by a long wall to reach The Lee. Turn right past The Cock & Rabbit to the green created by Sir Arthur Liberty, who lived at Lee Manor to the right.

Sir Arthur rented Lee Manor towards the end of the 19th century before purchasing the building in 1902. Once a year all the Regent Street staff were entertained to lunch and tea in the garden. Turn left to walk to the far end of the green and join the road for a short distance to reach the entrance to the churchyard. Arthur Liberty, who died in 1917, is buried in the Liberty plot to the right under an oak tree.

The Lee has two churches. The red brick one was built in 1869 but extensively rebuilt by Arthur Liberty who, as churchwarden, arranged for Liberty's to refurbish the interior. As patron of the living he appointed a relative to be Vicar. Continue past the church to the old church with its 13th-century walls leaning outwards. Until the Reformation it was served by monks from Missenden Abbey.

Go round the west end of the church to find a stile. At once go left over two further stiles by a house and bear half-right across the field to yet another stile. Here keep ahead over a junction to follow a track waymarked Chiltern Link. There is a hedge to the left, but after passing the end of a wood the hedge is to the right.

The path runs through a gap into another field. At the far end, turn left for a short distance to find a stile and continue north. There is a hedge to the right with a stile which should be ignored. Instead go over the stile at the end of the field and bear half-left to a stile and little gate at King's Ash Farm. Follow the drive round to reach the road and go straight over to a stile opposite.

Beyond a line of trees are two more stiles. Stay by the hedge on the left and after another stile by a wood continue in a semi-circle round the large field, staying close to the wood on the right. On eventually coming to a house, go over the stile and straight ahead past the front of the house. There is a garden with pool to the right before a stile is reached. Beyond here the path runs straight ahead and downhill through Concord Wood. Later, the path joins a sunken bridleway to the left just before meeting a junction. The way ahead is now part of the Ridgeway national trail, known here as Hogtrough Lane. After a cluster of houses there is a view to the right of Boddington Hill on the edge of Wendover Woods before the path drops down into a cutting.

After passing a farm and reaching Wellhead Cottage, cross the main road to go along Church Lane. This leads to Wendover Church, which is said to be outside the town due the original materials being mysteriously moved overnight. On seeing the back of the church, continue round the bend to find the lychgate entrance to the churchyard. The church has 14th-century work, although the exterior owes much to Victorian restoration. Go down Heron Path opposite the lychgate. The path swings right to Heron Cottage. Keep ahead, ignoring turnings, on a path which follows a stream for much of the way before reaching the town centre.

To the right is the clock tower, erected in 1842 and now the Tourist Information Centre. Ahead is unspoilt Aylesbury Road, flanked by attractive houses. To reach the station, go left up the High Street past The Red Lion and over a crossroads to turn right beside The Shoulder of Mutton.

Rainbow over Boddington Hill.

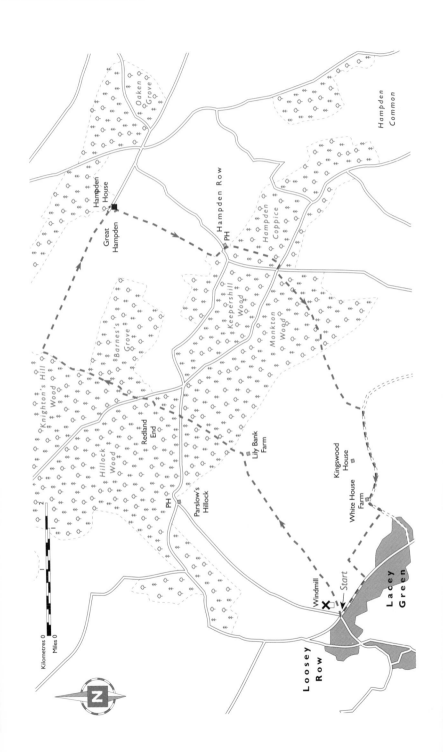

LACEY GREEN AND GREAT HAMPDEN

The Civil War which led to the execution of Charles I and a brief republic was fuelled by a stand on principle made by John Hampden from his then 600-year-old family country seat. Generations later, reference is made to Hampden in Grey's Elegy (Walk 11). This walk, from Lacey Green to the taxable land at Great Hampden and his mansion, starts by a windmill and follows a woodland trail which predates even the Hampdens arrival in the Chilterns.

Lacey Green is an old hamlet rather than a village and the church at the south end dates from only 1828. The walk starts at the north-west end of the main street by The Whip inn near the windmill. This, the oldest

INFORMATION

Distance: 10 km (6 miles).

Start and finish: The Whip at Lacey Green.

Terrain: Tracks and paths. Some sections can be muddy. Boots or strong shoes recommended.

Refreshments: Pubs at Lacey Green, Lily Bottom Lane and Hampden Row.

Public Transport: Rail to Princes Risborough then bus.

Opening hours: *Lacey Green Windmill:* May-Sept: Sun & Bank Hols 14.30-17.30. Admission charge.

Parslow's Hillock.

surviving smock mill, was built about 1650 at Chesham and moved here in 1821 where it was worked until 1915. It has recently been restored and is now in the hands of the Chiltern Society, whose members turn the sails on such special occasions as the annual National Mills Day. Visitors are welcome inside, to see the original massive machinery, on summer Sunday afternoons.

Go over the stile next to the bus shelter by The Whip. Follow the hedge to draw level with the windmill and cross a stile. The path runs ahead downhill and when the hedge on the left ends, the way is ahead across the field to another stile. Bear half right up to two stiles at the end of a fenced drove. Continue along an old field boundary to cross two more stiles and follow a fence on the right.

There is a wooden stile in the field corner by a gate. Go ahead into the next field, keeping to the left of the pylon to reach a wooden stile on the far side. Here there is a view half left over to The Pink & Lily pub at Parslow's Hillock. Walk half right across the corner of the field to a stile leading to Grim's Ditch.

The earthwork has always been a mystery, but is believed to be a Saxon boundary dating from the 8th century. The path here is outside the vast area which may at one time have been a territory surrounding

Hampden House.

Alyesbury. Grim's Ditch - which may mean 'Devil's Ditch'- is also found at Bradenham and south-east of Wendover. Bear left to walk down the Ditch, here a hollow lane, to a junction with Lily Bottom Lane. Turn left for a few yards to another junction.

Continue along the metalled Lily Bottom Lane to the junction with Wardrobes Lane only to visit The Pink & Lily. The pub is named after Mr Pink and Miss Lily, butler and maid at Hampden House, who retired to the cottage. The popular pub has been extended twice since Rupert Brooke was a regular visitor when walking here with his secret girlfriend Kathleen Nesbitt. The Brooke Bar is not a bar but the room the poet knew well with inglenook fireplace complete with rack for smoking hams. *The Chilterns*, a poem by Rupert Brooke featuring the pub in its opening lines, is displayed along with old photographs of the little pub. Appropriately, the ales available now include the local Chiltern Beechwood, and ham sandwiches are always on the menu.

The walk continues northwards by Lilybottom Farm and the cottage. Pass the cottage to the right and a turning right to keep ahead to a choice of paths. Take the left-hand bridleway which follows the line of Grim's Ditch, now over to the left. The path runs through the wood. There is a good view of the Ditch on the left as the path reaches a stile and gate. At a road junction, go ahead up the road marked 'Redland End' and 'Whiteleaf'. After a solitary house, the Pheasants, the road bends to reach Redland End hamlet.

At the T-junction go left for a very short distance then go right over a stile. Bear slightly left to go up on to the left bank of Grim's Ditch in a wood. Soon the path switches sides. Keep near the Ditch. On the far side of the trees a stile leads into a field. Keep ahead and in the next corner ignore the track to the left to keep forward. Ahead in the trees is a stile. Do not cross the stile, which is just before the point where the Ditch turns south-east.

Turn right, taking the footpath running beside a bridleway and through a long narrow avenue of ornamental pine trees planted by the Hampden Estate. At a field, the path crosses the parallel bridleway to continue inside the Ditch. Soon there is a small pond and later the path rejoins the bridleway. Ahead is a fine view of Hampden House.

The house, now a school, appears to be mid 18th-century gothic, but behind the facade is work dating from the 14th century. The family had been here since the Conquest when the famous John Hampden, a cousin of Oliver Cromwell, made a stand in 1637 against paying his one pound share of Ship Money tax which had been extended to inland areas (see page 95). As Member of Parliament for Buckinghamshire he played a leading role in the Parliamentary opposition to Charles I and was one of the five MPs who escaped arrest by taking a boat down the Thames just before the King entered the Commons chamber in 1642 to arrest them. Hampden subscribed £2000 to raise a regiment for the Roundhead army, and fought before being mortally wounded during a skirmish with Prince Rupert's troops at Chalgrove Field on 18 June 1643.

Go through the gateway and up the wide approach to Great Hampden. After a second gate there are castellated former stables to the right. Pass between the mansion and stable block to reach Great Hampden Church, which dates mainly from the same period as the house although the tower has a 13th-century doorway. Inside there is a 1476 brass to an earlier John Hampden as well as the large monument erected in 1743 showing the family tree sprouting out of the scene of John Hampden's battlefield death. His body lies outside and was dug up for examination in 1828 when the discovery of an amputated hand suggested that his death may have been due to an accident with his own firearm.

Leave the churchyard by the gate beyond the yew tree on the south side and follow the path running alongside a fence. Kissing gates take the path past a wooded pond and up to a burial mound at the top of the field. Just beyond a kissing gate, cross a metalled farm road and keep ahead along a now unmarked field boundary - the left-hand field is slightly lower. At an oak, the path follows a fence just inside a wood, with a view of houses at Hampden Row. Beyond a gateway, go ahead on a metalled road which bears left to a crossroads at Hampden Row. Across the road to the left is The Hampden Arms, a popular free house.

Go ahead over the crossroads, and just past the bus stop on the right, bear right along the side of the cricket ground. On the far side, go over the stile and into the wood. There is a hollow to the right before the path descends to a stile by gates at a road. Go right to a crossroads and up on a path on the left across the junction. The path turns sharp left uphill into Monkton Wood where there has been some recent felling and replanting. After crossing a main track the path has a parallel horseride to the left.

At the end of the wood go ahead on the narrow hedged bridleway between fields to meet the unmetalled Grubbins Lane - a continuation of Lily Bottom Lane. Keep forward on a still enclosed path which soon runs downhill to open out in a wood. Continue downhill on the now wider track through the trees to a T-junction below.

Footpath at Grubbins Lane.

Turn right along Speen Bottom - also known as Highwood Bottom - on a track called Kiln Lane. Up to the right is Kingswood House. Later there is the larger White House Farm. At a junction by the farm entrance, go left up the footpath. At a another junction turn right over a 'crossroads' and keep ahead by a house to enter a field. Still keep forward and at the far end find a view of the Lacey Green windmill. Turn left to follow a metalled road to the main village street.

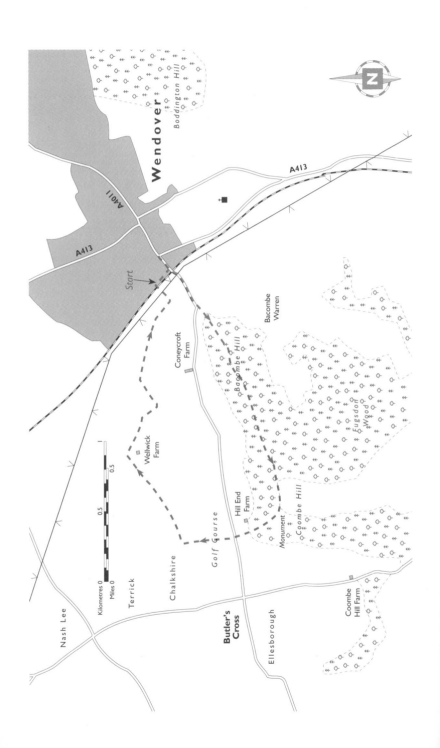

COOMBE HILL

Coombe Hill is the highest open space in the Chilterns; it affords a panoramic view north over Aylesbury, and on a clear day west as far as Wittenham Clumps on the Sinodun Hills 30 km (19 miles) away. The gentle climb out of Wendover is a very easy way of ascending 260 metres to this viewpoint. To avoid the steep path beyond the hilltop, you can return by the outward route which will be an easy downhill walk.

Turn right out of Wendover Station and go right again to cross the railway bridge. Follow the main road, which is part of the Ridgeway, by keeping to the pavement on the right in front of the cottages. Near the bend in the road cross over with care to keep ahead by taking the path up Bacombe Hill.

Where the way divides, keep right and at the next fork keep left to the kissing gate. Soon the way is up steps to a high path with a brief view to the north on the right. The path climbs gently on its way towards the top of Coombe Hill. Where the grass way widens out there are more views to the right. At the wood go through the wooden kissing gate - there is another up to the left. The path runs through the wood to bear left up to join the parallel path. A clear path runs ahead in the open.

Steps take the path down to cross a bridleway hollow and up to a kissing gate where the Coombe Hill monument can be seen ahead. This column is a Boer War memorial erected in 1904. From here, 260 m above the surrounding countryside, you can see Aylesbury Church tower 8 km to the north, Ivinghoe

INFORMATION

Distance: 6km (3 1/2 miles).

Start and finish: Wendover Station.

Terrain: Roads, tracks and paths. No special footwear needed.

Waymarked: Yes.

Refreshments: Several cafés and pubs in Wendover.

Coombe Hill monument.

Beacon (the next high point on the Ridgeway) to the east and just to the south-west the woods of Chequers. Lord Lee, who gave Chequers for the use of Prime Ministers, also gave this viewpoint to the National Trust in 1918.

The walk continues from the north side of the monument. Go half left down the grass ridge. Soon the ground falls very steeply. Go downhill and ahead between the trees. Beyond a barrier there is a view to the left of a golf course and, ahead, a gate leading to a road which cuts through Ellesborough Golf Club.

Go directly across the road and keep ahead past a building on the right. Still continue ahead - there are plenty of signs - to reach a stile on the far side of the golf course. Continue forward for only a short distance. On coming level with a stile on the left, go sharp right across the open field. This is part of the 50 km-long Aylesbury Ring trail which circles the town but is never more than five miles from it. The Ring waymarking can be found on the next two stiles.

View North from Coombe Hill.

View North from Coombe Hill.

Once in the orchard at Wellwick Farm, look for the well-marked stile to the left. Beyond here is a good view to the right of the house dating from 1616. The south front is now early Georgian, but on the north side the successive additions can clearly be seen. The chimneys are the most distinctive feature.

Just beyond the north side, bear half-right following the waymarks on the two telegraph poles. The way is down into the dip to a stile by a wide gateway. Beyond the stile, go ahead and over the metalled roadway. There is a barn to the right. At once go left to find a waymark on yet another telegraph pole. Turn right, as indicated, to walk south-east along a fenceless field boundary. Beyond a bend there is a stile. Cross the stile to follow the fence on the left. Here there is a view back to the house at Wellwick Farm.

At the far end, the path cuts the field corner to a stile. Ahead is a direct path to a railway bridge, but the walk goes half-right (with the Aylesbury Ring) towards Wendover Station. At a field corner outside a playing field, bear right along the boundary with the playing field to the left. Where an upright sleeper indicates a crosspath, go left along the inside of the playing field to a stile on the far side. A short path ahead leads directly to the footbridge at Wendover Station.

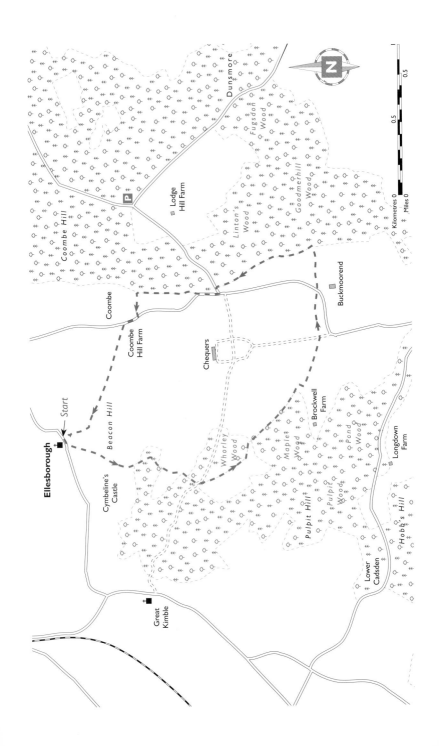

ELLESBOROUGH AND CHEQUERS

I n 1921, when Lord Lee gave his home Chequers as a country residence for the Prime Minister, he wrote: "...the better the health of our rulers the more sanely they will rule, and the inducement to spend two days a week in the high and pure air of the Chiltern hills and woods will, it is hoped, benefit the nation as well as its chosen leaders". Clement Attlee so loved the place that when he retired he lived nearby. This walk explores the estate where premiers have found refreshment and peace.

The route starts at Ellesborough Church, where Prime Ministers have worshipped and often read the lesson. As the figures above the porch indicate it is dedicated to St Peter and St Paul - there are even St Peter's and St Paul's Cottages on the eastern side of the churchyard. Most of the building is mid-Victorian but there has been a church on this high ground for centuries and inside there is 14th-century work.

INFORMATION

Distance: 6km (3 1/2 miles).

Start and finish: Ellesborough Church.

Terrain: Roads, tracks and paths. Some sections can be muddy after wet weather, in which case strong footwear is advised.

Waymarked: Yes.

Public Transport: Rail to Aylesbury or Princes Risborough then bus.

Parking: Parking space is severely limited at the church. Those arriving by car should park at Butler's Cross to the east and walk along the road to Ellesborough Church. There is a pavement which turns into a footpath to run directly into the churchyard.

Refreshments: The Russell Arms at Butler's Cross.

Ellesborough Church.

Leave the churchyard by the double gate and go down the slope to cross the road. At the bus stop, go right along a short path leading to a kissing gate. The path can be seen running half-right across the field. Once on the far side, go over the stile in the band of trees to continue in the same direction.

To the left is Beacon Hill - probably named after an heraldic device of the Hawtrey family, who owned Chequers for more than 300 years until 1597. To the right is a site known as Cymbeline's Castle, said to have been a fort built by the British King Cunobelinus, who died about AD 43. As the path begins to curve back towards the fence on the left there is a view to the right over the wooded Ellesborough Warren. After a stile, the way is soon up steps to reach open ground. Keep forward to find a path curving through the trees ahead. Cross the metalled western driveway to Chequers at an angle and climb over the stile by the usually open gate.

Ignore all turnings off to the right across the huge field and stay by the fence of Whorley Wood on the left. At the far end join the Ridgeway national trail to go through a kissing gate, by a white wooden farm gate, for a first view of Chequers and the two gazebos in the Rose Garden. Turn right along the side of Maple Wood on a path which provides a splendid view of the Elizabethan manor house in its sheltered Chiltern hollow.

In the 12th century the earlier house had belonged to an Exchequer official whose family took the name 'de Chekers', which led to today's Chequers. In the new Tudor house Lady Mary Grey, Lady Jane's sister, was held prisoner for two years for marrying a servant without Royal permission. The first Prime Minister to take up residence was Lloyd George. Only Bonar Law declined to use Chequers. Churchill spent crucial hours here in the war and recent premiers including Wilson, Callaghan and Thatcher invited foreign statesmen here for talks. Harold Wilson even held cabinet meetings at the house.

After the path bears south, continue for only a short distance before going over a stile on the left. From here the path runs ahead gently downhill to a series of kissing gates which take the path over the main driveway and near the lodges. The avenue of beech trees was presented by the Churchill family in 1955 in memory of his "momentous days" spent here.

Harvest time at Chequers.

The way continues ahead to turn to a kissing gate by the road. Cross over and take the left track signposted 'Ridgeway'. After a short distance, be sure to watch for the waymark to avoid walking into a field. Soon the track briefly divides to offer a less muddy surface through the beech wood. At a four-way junction, go left on a path which runs north near the edge of the wood for 800 m.

At a road, turn left to a T-junction and go right to pass a Chequers estate lodge. Here go right on to a footpath which continues north as the road runs down to the north-west. Keep right at an early divide but at the

Coombe Hill Farm.

next fork go down to the left on a path paved with tree roots. Go left again to pass, after a modern house, between Coombe Hill Farm Cottage and the long building of Coombe Hill Farm and reach the road. Turn right along the road in front of the farmhouse. After a short distance cross the road to barriers at the start of a long footpath running up a large field.

The 800 m path eventually runs alongside a short field boundary before meeting barriers at a track linking Chequers with Ellesborough Church. Turn right to follow the track down to the road. The church is opposite.

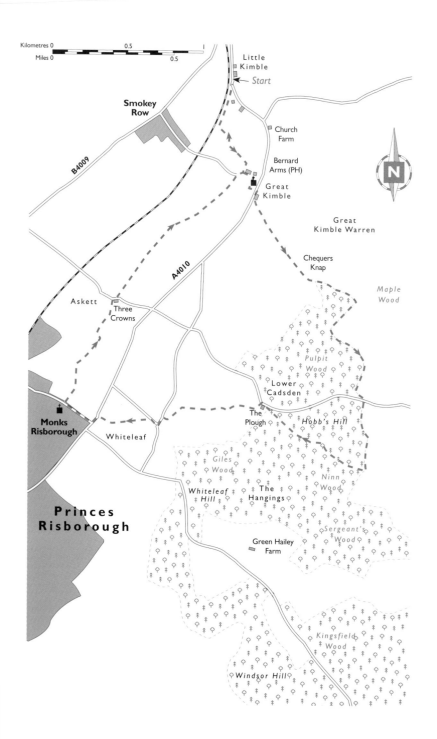

Kilometres 0   0.5   1
Miles 0   0.5

Little
Kimble
← *Start*

**Smokey
Row**

Church
Farm

B4009

Bernard
Arms (PH)

**Great
Kimble**

N

Great
Kimble Warren

Chequers
Knap

*Maple
Wood*

A4010

*Pulpit
Wood*

Askett

Three
Crowns

Lower
Cadsden

The
Plough

Hobb's Hill

**Monks
Risborough**

Whiteleaf

*Giles
Wood*

*Ninn
Wood*

*Whiteleaf
Hill*

**The
Hangings**

**Princes
Risborough**

*Sergeant's
Wood*

Green Hailey
Farm

*Kingsfield
Wood*

Windsor Hill

GREAT KIMBLE AND MONKS RISBOROUGH

Great Kimble is a quiet village, but its church was once the scene of a far-reaching meeting. This walk also passes through an ancient village which once belonged to Canterbury by way of woodland and farmland.

From Little Kimble Station, turn right to find the start of an enclosed footpath. Beyond a stile the path enters a field. Keep forward by the hedge as far as the stile on the right leading down on to the railway. Do not cross the stile but go left across the field to a short fenced approach to a gateway by a stream.

Go over the stile to pass a large pond and keep half-right to go over a series of three stiles to reach the

INFORMATION

Distance: 8km (5 miles).

Start and finish: Little Kimble Station.

Terrain: Roads, tracks and paths. Some sections can be muddy in wet weather but special footwear is not normally needed.

Refeshments: The Bernard Arms at Great Kimble and The Three Crowns at Askett.

Great Kimble church sign.

school at Great Kimble. The path passes through the playground to go down the far side of the main building. At the road, go left to pass a cottage with a well and reach a junction flanked by the church and pub.

St Nicholas Church has a splendid sign depicting the patron saint of children in the churchyard. It was in 1637, in this mainly 14th-century church, which has a Norman font from an earlier building, that John Hampden announced his refusal to pay Ship Money and so moved the country towards the Civil War (see also Walk 19). The tax had been imposed on ports and coastal counties prior to the Spanish Armada invasion threat but Charles I's attempt to extend it inland as a tax only nominally for defence led to the resistance.

The Bernard Arms was once called The Chequers which would be appropriate today since customers have included Prime Ministers from nearby Chequers. Harold Wilson called in for a lunchtime pint on his last Sunday in office and John Major brought President Yeltsin of Russia here to see a typical English pub. Lobby journalists have been briefed at the bar following ministerial talks at the premier's country house.

Turn right to pass the church and after a short distance go left up a track passing between the white Pickade House and a thatched cottage. The track climbs to give first a view south to Chinnor Hill. Soon there is a view to the left towards Aylesbury. After a short distance there is a crosspath in the woods. Here turn right over a low bank to enter Pulpit Wood.

Soon the wooded ground falls away to the right. To the left are the earthworks of an iron age fort. Ignore any left turns and shortly there is a view down on to Great Kimble's church and pub. The high path bears right. Here go left as the arrow indicates on a path which bears left to run in a straight line through the beeches. At a crosspath turn right downhill to a stile and bear left along a track. Cross a road to go down a bridleway opposite.

Sheep near Monks Risborough.

Here there is a parallel path for those wanting to avoid mud. At a junction keep right and at once go over a stile into a wood. Go ahead but keep right at a divide to go down through new planting. On meeting a substantial track go right. The track curves downhill. At a junction keep ahead to reach The Plough.

Go past the pub to find a footpath on the left just past Plough Farm. The path runs up to a stile and remains enclosed as far as a thatched cottage. Beyond a stile go over a track and ahead across a golf course to a kissing gate leading to a cricket field. Bear to the left past the pavilion and on to the metalled road. Just before a house called Woodpecker go left along a footpath.

On emerging at a residential enclave, go right to reach the road. Turn left and then right down The Holloway. Just beyond a driveway on the left go up a footpath. The enclosed way runs to a kissing gate. Continue across a field to another kissing gate

and walk up the side of Monks Risborough Primary School to a third kissing gate. Go left along the road and right at the war memorial into Mill Lane.

To visit the church go left down Burton Lane and first right. 'Monks' in the village name is a reminder that the village once belonged to Canterbury Cathedral; the church is dedicated to St Dunstan, who was Archbishop of Canterbury from 959 to 988 and is depicted in a north aisle window. Continue past the church to return to the road and find a footpath entrance opposite.

Those staying in Mill Lane will find the foopath on the right just before Courtmoor Close. The path runs to a stile behind buildings. Bear half-left over a field towards a stile but do not go over it. Instead, continue up the left side of the field to go over a series of three stiles. The path runs ahead by a wall on the left. At a garden go left through a gate and along an enclosed way to find Meadowcroft Farmhouse. Follow the lane to a junction at Askett.

Turn right to The Three Crowns. By the pub sign go left to a stile. Keep ahead up the field and over a series of stiles through four fields. At the final stile in a corner, continue in the northerly direction. Two further stiles takes the path over the driveway by a rustic shed. Cross a field to a stile where the path divides. Keep slightly left to go over the field, which has earthworks, and find a stile by a set-back gate. There are lakes to the left. Follow the firm path ahead which later turns a corner to a stile above the road in Great Kimble.

Go right up the road and turn left into the school to follow the outward route back to Little Kimble Station.

Opposite: Cottage in Great Kimble.

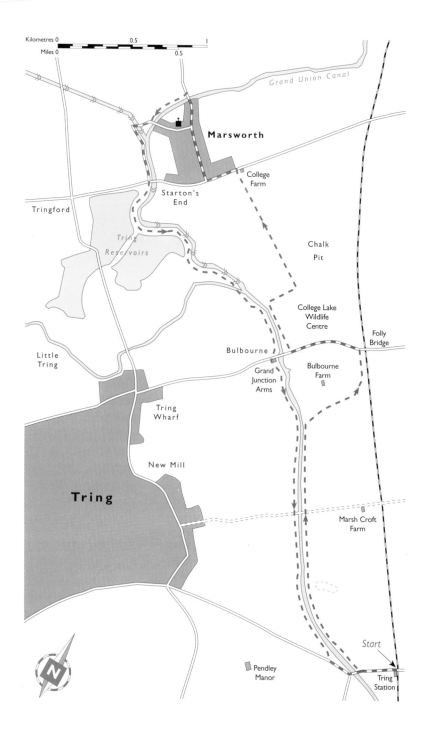

Kilometres 0   0.5   1

Miles 0   0.5

Grand Union Canal

Marsworth

College Farm

Starton's End

Tringford

Tring Reservoirs

Chalk Pit

College Lake Wildlife Centre

Folly Bridge

Little Tring

Bulbourne

Bulbourne Farm

Grand Junction Arms

Tring Wharf

New Mill

Tring

Marsh Croft Farm

Start

Pendley Manor

Tring Station

MARSWORTH

The Grand Union Canal, featured on this walk, dates from 1793, and the route takes advantage of less known paths near the canal as well as lakes, locks and an interesting waterway junction at Marsworth. The canal village maintains the old tradition of feeding the long-distance traveller by having three charming free house pubs.

Tring Station is next to The Royal Hotel, which describes itself as a 'posting house'. The station and hotel both opened in 1838 to serve Tring, 2 km to the west. To the east can be seen the tall Bridgewater Monument commemorating the 3rd Duke of Bridgewater, 'Father of Inland Navigation', who financed two canals in the 1760s.

From the station turn left to pass The Royal Hotel and walk as far as the canal bridge. This road is part of the Ridgeway national trail. Do not cross the water but go right to steps leading down to the towpath. Only go down a few steps before turning up to the right on a path which runs high above the canal path. Beyond a cottage garden the way is soon fenced as it runs along the side of a field. To the right is a view of Pitstone Hill. Keep by the side of the field to pass through a band of woodland. Beyond here the path is again fenced and there is view of the tall chimney at Pitstone chalk pit. At the far end the path runs down a few steps to the Marshcroft Lane canal bridge.

Cross the road, not the canal, to continue north on another fenced path. After passing a recently created pond, the way bears round to the right. When the fencing ends keep forward through trees and beyond a track keep to the hedge on the left. Closely planted trees have created new field boundaries here. At a stile, go half-left up a sloping field towards the tall chimney to find the railway in a cutting. Follow the top of the embankment to a stile by Folly Bridge on Upper Icknield Way - the original Ridgeway. Turn left along the road where traffic is slowed by the lights at

INFORMATION

Distance: 11km (6 1/2 miles).

Start and Finish: Tring Station.

Terrain: Roads, paths and towpath. The paths can be muddy after rain, and in such conditions strong footwear is advised.

Refreshments: Hotel at Tring Station. Waterside Pubs at Marsworth.

the narrow bridge. This is also the county boundary, with Hertforshire to the left and Buckinghamshire on the right.

Walk on the right-hand side of the road; after a bend the entrance to College Lake Wildlife Centre overlooks the flooded Pitstone chalk pit, which for over 40 years until 1991 provided chalk for Castle cement works. There is a covered historic farm trail with live animals as well as a fund-raising second-hand bookshop.

Continue along the road and before the canal go right along a signposted path. The way soon runs gently downhill through an avenue of tall trees and is near the canal just before turning right. After a double bend the path is lined by hedges as it runs straight for 1 km towards Marsworth. Over to the left can be seen

Marsworth Church Gate.

Wendover Woods on Aston Hill beyond Tring. After passing a barn there is a T-junction with Lower Icknield Way.

Cross the road and go left to pass The Crescent. Turn right down Vicarage Road. The castellated tower of Marsworth Church can be seen at the end. The south aisle is the old church which was widened in the 14th century. Its Victorian restoration was undertaken by the Vicar, who trained villagers as stonemasons. This DIY tradition continues with the altar rail kneelers and the dossal cloth behind being designed and made locally in 1971 and 1980. The painting of the pregnant Virgin Mary is by the children's illustrator Jan Pienkowski, who allowed Marsworth children to paint the border.

Continue ahead with the church to the left downhill to pass The Red Lion and cross the canal. Go left over a stile to join the towpath, and keep ahead with the water to the left. As the canal bears round to the left you see the Old Manor, a white timber-framed building dating from the early Tudor period. At the

Signpost at Marsworth canal junction.

next bridge go up to the road and turn right to take the left fork. After a short distance the lane crosses the Aylesbury Arm of the Grand Union.

Look left from the bridge to see two narrow locks joined together to form a staircase. To the right, seven conventional locks follow in quick succession taking the canal towards the county town of Buckinghamshire, 10 km away. This arm opened in 1814 as part of an unfullfilled plan to continue to Abingdon.

Continue over the bridge, go right to reach the towpath and go right again under the road and past the locks. The towpath leads back to the Grand Union on a stretch which has a towpath on both sides. Moored ahead outside The White Lion you may see the narrowboat Wylo with Derek Pearson, fender and chimney maker, sitting on the towpath making ropes.

Cross the road to the first of seven locks on the snaking Marsworth Flight, known to regular users as Maffers. Here the bridge can be seen to have a double arch, recalling 1838 when a duplicate lock was planned as part of a reaction to the threat of the new speedy railways. Soon the path is just below the Tring Reservoirs, built to feed the canal but now run as a nature reserve. Tufted duck, pochard and shoveler can be seen here. At the bend take the parallel high path as far as the lock for a view across the wide waters. Between the third and fourth lock there is a good view across the reservoir backwater where herons can sometimes be seen.

The flight of locks ends at a dry dock opposite the Wendover Arm, which opened in 1797 although the leaky chalk means that it no longer runs its full length. Here the attractive junction is known as the Tring Summit Level. Cross the bridge over the arm to follow the main towpath round a bend to the Grand Junction Arms at Bulbourne. At the British Waterways workshop you may see new wooden lock gates soaking in the water.

Pass under the Upper Icknield Way Bridge and out of Buckinghamshire. The way now in Hertfordshire is soon wooded as the canal runs through a deep cutting which offers cool relief in summer but can be cold at other times. At Marshcroft Lane the towpath crosses the bridge. However, the walk stays on the same bank by continuing ahead up a few steps to run parallel with the canal along the edge of four fields.

Just before the far end of the last field is a white house, which should be kept to the right. Go left down a few steps and follow an enclosed way, passing the house to the right. At the road, go left to a junction where the road joins the Ridgeway Path to cross the canal. Ahead is Tring Station.

Canal at Tring reservoirs.

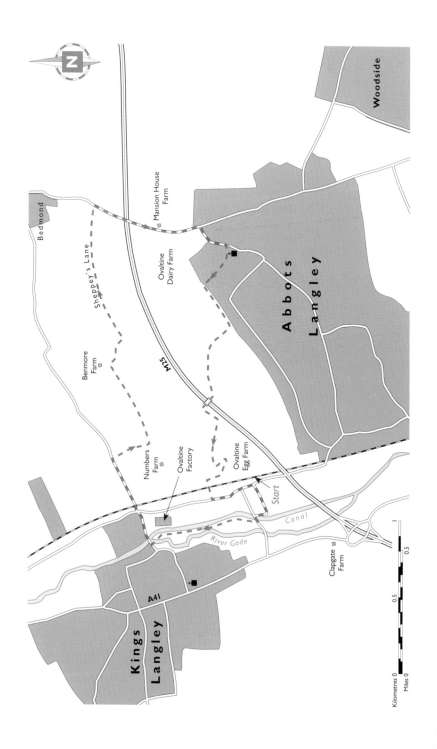

Woodside

Bedmond

Sheppey's Lane

Mansion House Farm

Ovaltine Dairy Farm

Benmore Farm

M25

Abbots Langley

Numbers Farm

Ovaltine Factory

Ovaltine Egg Farm

Start

Canal

River Gade

Clapgate Farm

A41

Kings Langley

Kilometres 0   0.5   1
Miles 0   0.5

OVALTINE FARM

The famous Ovaltine drink was launched in Switzerland in 1904 by Dr George Wander, who was researching the nutritional values of barley malt. In 1913 the company built a factory at Kings Langley in the Gade Valley below its 460-acre farm which until 1979 produced milk and eggs for the production. For many years the Ovaltine diary maid appeared on every tin. This walk explores the Ovaltine farmland, which was once the childhood playground of the only Englishman to become Pope.

From Kings Langley Station, turn right and just beyond the bus stop, go left down a metalled footpath to cross a mill stream. On meeting the Grand Union Canal (also the River Gade), the way turns right. Cross the canal bridge and at once go right down steps on to the towpath.

Turn left to go under the two bridges and past a lock. The Gade flows separately on the left of the towpath which is just in Buckinghamshire, while the far canal bank is in Hertfordshire. Soon there is a milestone reading 'Braunston 68' - this refers to a major canal junction in Warwickshire. There is usually a distinctive smell floating across the water from the

INFORMATION

Distance: 6km (4 miles).

Start and finish: Kings Langley Station.

Terrain: Road, track and path. No special footwear needed.

Refreshments: Wide choice at Kings Langley and Abbots Langley.

Public Transport: Kings Langley is on the North London Railways Euston-Birmingham line.

Lock at King's Langley.

Ovaltine factory, which was built beside the canal so that Ovaltine barges could bring coal from the Midlands to the back door.

Over to the left can be seen Kings Langley, which was once called Chiltern Langley. The present name recalls the now disappeared royal palace but the church contains the tomb of Edmund Langley, the first Duke of York, and his wife Isabel of Castile. Also in the church is a brass of John Carter, ancestor of former US President Jimmy Carter. A Carter helped to rebuild Edward III's palace here and as late as the 17th century a member of the family was Vicar.

At the bridge, cross the road and look north to see the canal divide - one course is the former channel, replaced in 1818. Continue over the bridge to walk away from the village to a road junction. Go up Tom's Lane opposite, keeping on the left-hand side until after the railway bridge. Then walk on the right-hand side until joining a pavement set back from the main traffic. Just beyond number 78, go through gates to follow a footpath into a field.

The path runs downhill, with a view of the factory in the valley, and uphill to join a track at a bend. Turn left on the wide path, known as Sheppey's Lane. After a belt of trees there is a brief view up to Abbots Langley Church beyond the M25 motorway. There are several bends before the way climbs up towards the edge of Bedmond, birthplace in 1100 of Nicholas Breakspear. He took holy orders at Avignon in France, and in 1152 was sent by the then pope, Eugenius III, to reorganise the church in Scandinavia, earning the title 'Apostle of the North'. In 1154 Breakspear was elected Pope and took the name Adrian IV. Until his death in 1159 he was engaged in a fierce struggle for power in Europe with the Holy Roman Emperor, Frederick I, known as Barbarossa.

Just before the path is enclosed by hedges there is a view over to the right of the former Ovaltine Diary Farm. On meeting a road turn right away from Bedmond. After crossing the M25 the road passes the thatched Ovaltine Dairy Farm, built in 1935. The half-timbered building and circular dairy were both converted into housing in 1982-4. Continue ahead to pass Abbots Langley School and turn right to walk into the village.

Outside the library is a Hertfordshire Pudding Stone, dug up when the M25 was being cut through here in 1986. St Lawrence's Church, also the parish church of Bedmond, was built in the early 12th century, when Nicholas Breakspear was a child. Inside, a plaque records his election to the Papacy. His father was employed by St Alban's Abbey, which owned the farmland east of the River Gade - hence 'Abbots' Langley.

Turn into the church-yard and take the path running north behind the church, keeping left where the way divides, to follow a wall. The path runs between gardens and over a road to reach fields. Turn left to follow the fence along the back

Abbots Langley Church.

gardens. The Chiltern hills can be seen ahead above Kings Langley. At a junction turn right to meet a farm track at a bend.

Go left to follow the way downhill, passing a cottage hidden in trees, to cross a bridge high over the M25. The now metalled way bears left to run gently downhill to pass the former Ovaltine Egg Farm, which once housed 30,000 pullets. The main circular building, looking like a film set, is over to the left and a little further on there is the farm entrance where the words 'Ovaltine Egg Farm' can just be discerned over the gateway. The field to the south, now cut by the M25, would once have been dotted with poultry huts.

Follow the road downhill and under the railway line. Turn left along the main road to Kings Langley Station.

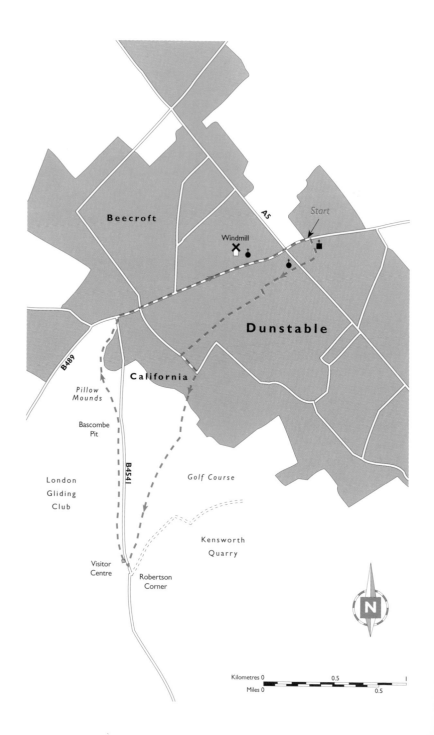

Beecroft

A5

Start

Windmill

Dunstable

B489

California

*Pillow
Mounds*

Bascombe
Pit

B4541

London
Gliding
Club

Golf Course

Visitor
Centre

Robertson
Corner

Kensworth
Quarry

N

Kilometres 0   0.5   1
Miles 0   0.5

DUNSTABLE DOWNS

enry I founded Dunstable Priory on the road from London to the north in the 12th century. In 1533, the Augustinian priory church proved a handy country location for staging the court hearing which provided Henry VIII with his marriage annulment. Freed from Catherine of Aragon, he not only brought his new wife Anne Boleyn here, but went on to honeymoon in the town with later wives Catherine Howard and Catherine Parr.

This walk starts at the impressive cathedral-like priory church, where its Henry window appropriately includes a broken lovers' knot, and takes a pleasant route up on to the Downs for spectacular views enjoyed by the priory monks when they farmed rabbits on the viewpoint.

Leaving the west door of the Priory, turn left through a gateway into Priory Meadow and follow the path which bears right to reach another gateway at the side of Priory House. This was the pilgrim lodging belonging to the monastery which also owned the Saracen's Head along to the left. Its unusually long frontage is due to the fact that it was three pubs - the George, the Saracen's Head and the Bell. Opposite is The Square with High Street South, part of the Roman built Watling Street, running through it. Cross the road, using the crossing along to the right, and walk up the side of the Methodist church opposite.

INFORMATION

Distance: 6km
(4 miles).

Start and finish:
Dunstable Priory
Church.

Terrain: Roads,
tracks and paths. No
special footwear
needed.

Refreshments: Wide
choice including old
inns in Dunstable.
Refreshment kiosk at
Information Centre on
Downs.

Public Transport:
Bus from Luton
Station.

Dunstable Priory.

Continue ahead across a large car park to emerge by the Salvation Army building on Bull Pond Lane. Go left for a few yards and then right into the Bennett Memorial Recreation Ground. Follow the path, with a glimpse of the Downs ahead. At the far end, cross Canesworde Road to go up a rough lane. Later, beyond allotments, the way is metalled. At a junction, do not go ahead past the post boxes but turn left. At another junction, opposite a school, turn right. Where the road swings left, keep ahead up a lane.

Dunstable Downs.

The way is uphill. At a fork, go ahead on a narrow path which also runs uphill. Ignore a left turning where there is a view. Soon the way runs on to a golf course. Aim for a point just left of the clubhouse. On the way there are fine views back down on to Dunstable. The large tower blocks are next to the source of the River Lee which runs down the east side of London. There are two posts near the clubhouse. On reaching a car park, follow the yellow lines which mark the public footpath. The way continues over grass between young trees with fine views each side. After passing through woodland, the path reaches a road on top of the Downs.

Cross and turn right to drop down to the Visitor Centre, which is 800 feet above sea level. Sometimes gliders float low overhead before plunging down to the grass airfield below. Once, sheep on this chalk grassland would have kept the scrub in check without modern management which protects the rich abundance of wild flowers. Birds include the common skylark.

Continue beyond the Centre and parallel with the road over to the right. After a gate, the way begins to climb up round Bascombe Pit, with a dramatic drop on the left and panoramic views. Just beyond here, to the left, are to the 'Pillow Mounds'. These sometimes hard to discern bumps - the largest is 32 metres long - are 13th-century rabbit warrens built by Dunstable Priory monks to supply meat and fur. The Normans had brought rabbits over from Normandy at the Conquest. A warrener lived on site and either sent dogs inside, or smoked out a passage, before catching the required number of rabbits in a net.

The path continues ahead and after a gate continues downhill and across the grass to a road junction. Opposite is Drovers' Way, once used for bringing sheep to market in Dunstable. Turn right along the West Street main road running into Dunstable. This road is part of the ancient Icknield Way, a continuation of the Ridgeway. Before you reach the centre of Dunstable there is a view of a windmill, built in 1839 with local grey bricks, behind St Mary's Church on the left.

Glider above Dunstable Downs.

INDEX

Opposite: Looking towards Turville from Summerheath Wood.

Other titles in this series

25 Walks – In and Around Aberdeen
25 Walks – In and Around Belfast
25 Walks – The Cotswolds
25 Walks – Deeside
25 Walks – Dumfries and Galloway
25 Walks – Edinburgh and Lothian
25 Walks – Fife
25 Walks – In and Around Glasgow
25 Walks – Highland Perthshire
25 Walks – The Scottish Borders
25 Walks – The Trossachs
25 Walks – The Yorkshire Dales

Other titles in preparation

25 Walks – In Argyll (Arrochar, Cowal and Bute)
25 Walks – Down
25 Walks – Fermanah
25 Walks – In and Around London

Long distance guides published by The Stationery Office

The West Highland Way – Official Guide
The Southern Upland Way – Official Guide

Published by The Stationery Office and available from:

The Stationery Office Bookshops
71 Lothian Road, Edinburgh EH3 9AZ
(counter service only)
South Gyle Crescent, Edinburgh EH12 9EB
(mail, fax and telephone orders only)
0131-479 3141 Fax 0131-479 3142
49 High Holborn, London WC1V 6HB
(counter service and fax orders only)
Fax 0171-831 1326
68-69 Bull Street, Birmingham B4 6AD
0121-236 9696 Fax 0121-236 9699
33 Wine Street, Bristol BS1 2BQ
0117-926 4306 Fax 0117-929 4515
9-21 Princess Street, Manchester M60 8AS
0161-834 7201 Fax 0161-833 0634
16 Arthur Street, Belfast BT1 4GD
01232 238451 Fax 01232 235401
The Stationery Office Oriel Bookshop
The Friary, Cardiff CF1 4AA
01222 395548 Fax 01222 384347

The Stationery Office publications are also available from:

The Publications Centre
(mail, telephone and fax orders only)
PO Box 276, London SW8 5DT
General enquiries 0171-873 0011
Telephone orders 0171-873 9090
Fax orders 0171-873 8200

Printed in Scotland for The Stationery Office by CC No. 70343 50c 11/96